Praise for Treasures from the Spirit World

Rev. Karen Heasley has compiled an encyclopedia of information regarding Spiritualism. Whether new to Spiritualism or not, this comprehensive book explains and gives insight into the history and philosophy of this religion in a way that is easy to read and understand. Having her own personal story intertwined throughout the book, Rev. Heasley shows the reader how a new experience, or class, or thought can shift our path and allow us to open our own gifts and potential. Her church, radio show, blogs, and now this book are testaments to following our heart and building on the past to create the future.

Rev. Sharon Siubis
Inner Spiritual Center, Fairfield NJ

Rev. Heasley has reintroduced the foundation of Spiritualism for the novice, in a easy to grasp format. To the current participant she has reawakened our understanding of eternal life, and to the elders, a fresh reminder that life is an advancement of truth, love and deeds. Brought forth to all in a very welcomed time for healing.

Rev. Barbara Sanson
President of the Lily Dale Healing Association

Rev. Heasley has captured in this book 'Gems' of our Spiritualist Truths, History, and our science. Presented in a readable style for contemporary minds. The information in this book should be part of the foundational knowledge for every seeker of Spiritualist truth. A must read for the serious student.

Rev. Eileen V. Montgomery, DCP
Spiritualist and seeker since 1959

Treasures from the Spirit World not only opens the door to the Novice just beginning their Spiritual Journey but expands further on the knowledge of those already on their Spiritual Path. Rev. Karen discusses not only what Spiritualism is but also discusses the mysteries of the Spirit World and Mediumship, Spirit Guides, Angels and also addresses some of the misconceptions about the soul's journey to the Spirit World. Rev. Karen's book is an easy read for all.

Rev. Carole Boyce
Inner Spiritual Center

I have been a practicing Spiritualist for over 40 years and have read many volumes on numerous aspects of Spiritualism. Treasures from the Spirit World is a wonderful overview of the history, philosophy, and practices of modern Spiritualism. The truly inspirational aspects of the religion are presented along with the phenomenal and sometimes controversial exploits of celebrated mediums. I would happily direct anyone with an interest in the subject of Spiritualism to this work.

Rev. Tom Cratsley
Associate Director of Fellowships
Spirit School of Healing and Prophesy

Treasures from the Spirit World

Reverend Karen L. Heasley
with
Susan Urbanek Linville

TREASURES FROM THE SPIRIT WORLD

Copyright 2018 by Karen L. Heasley and Susan Urbanek Linville

All rights reserved.

Published Pokeberry Press, a division of Pokeberry Exchange, LLC., New Castle, Pennsylvania

www.pokeberryexchange.com

No part of this book may be used or reproduced in any manner whatsoever without written permission except in the case of brief quotations embodied in critical reviews and articles. For information, Pokeberry Press, 41 N. Mercer St., New Castle, Pennsylvania 16101

Pokeberry books may be purchased for book club, educational, business, and promotional use. For information, email editor@pokeberryexchange.com with your request.

ISBN 978-0-9972276-6-6

Printed in the United States of America

Cover Art – Precipitated Artwork supplied by Reverend Leonard Young. Origin of the painting is unknown.

Book Design by Stephen V. Ramey

Contents

Dedication i
Foreword i
INTRODUCTION iii
Section I: THE RELIGION OF SPIRITUALISM 1
  What Spiritualism is and is Not. 1
  Affiliation Should Not Divide Us 3
  The Spirit World: All Around Us 5
  Spheres of the Spirit World 7
  The Titanic Sinking from the Other Side 10
  Passing Over to the Other Side 12
  Spirit Guides Part I: Silver Birch 15
  Spirit Guides Part II: Choo Chow 18
  Spirit Guides Part III: Maurice de la Tour 20
  Spirit Guides Part IV: Light 22
  Spirit Guides Part V: Red Cloud 25
  The Ministry of Angels 27
  Personal Responsibility 30
  A Life of Giving Thanks: Part I 32
  A Life of Giving Thanks: Part II 34
  A Religion of Self-Mastery 36
  A Religion of Introspection 38
  A Religion of Lifting Self and Others. 40

Spirits Do Not Get Stuck	42
Spiritualism in Today's World	44
Have We Lived Here Before?	47
Halloween and Spiritualism	50
Section II: THE HISTORY OF SPIRITUALISM	**53**
Hydesville, NY: Part I	55
Hydesville, NY: Part II	57
Hydesville, NY: Part III	59
Hydesville, NY: Part IV	62
National Spiritualist Association of Churches	65
Spiritualists' National Union	68
International Spiritualist Federation	70
Arthur Findlay College	72
Colored Spiritualist Association of Churches	74
Lily Dale: Home to Spiritualism	76
Lily Dale: A Place of Magic	78
International Women's Day: Women Spiritualists	81
Precipitated Spirit Paintings: Part I	84
Precipitated Spirit Paintings: Part II	86
Spirit Photography: Part I	88
Spirit Photography: Part II	91
Spirit Photography: Part III	96
Spirit Photography: Part IV	98
The Scole Experiment	100
Section III: NOTABLE PEOPLE	**103**
Mother Leafy Anderson: African American Medium	105

Albert (Wishart) Best: Trance Medium 107

Helena Blavatsky: The Theosophical Society 110

Mina (Margery) Crandon: Physical Medium 112

Emma Hardinge Britten and the Seven Principles 115

Sir Arthur Conan Doyle: Author and Spiritualist 119

Andrew Jackson Davis: The Poughkeepsie Seer 121

Leslie Flint: Direct Voice Medium 123

Harry Edwards: Spiritual Healer 125

Geoffrey Hodson: Angels, Spirits and Fairies. 127

Allan Kardec: Father of Spiritism 129

Helen Keller: Swedenborg Follower 132

Robert James Lees: Boy Medium 134

J. Hewat McKenzie: Parapsychology Researcher 136

Vice-Admiral W. Usborne Moore: Unbeliever Turned Believer. 138

Eusapia Palladino: Physical Medium or Trickster? 141

Coral Polge: Psychic Artist 144

Morris Pratt: Institute Builder 146

Paschal Beverly Randolph: African American Trance Medium 148

Charles Richet: Ectoplasm 150

Theodate Pope Riddle: Pioneer, Architect and Spiritualist. 152

Mary S. Vanderbilt: Devoted Spiritualist 154

Etta Wriedt: Spirit Voice Medium 156

Section IV: THE PRACTICE OF SPIRITUALISM 159

Finding your Silence 161

Forget Yourself and Grow 163
Angels in Our Lives 165
It's Supposed to be the Most Wonderful Time of the Year .. 167
Visiting a Medium: What to Expect 169
Harry Edwards' Thoughts on Mediumship 171
Beginning Mediumship 173
Developing A Mediumship Circle: Part 1 175
Developing a Mediumship Circle: Part II 177
Physical Mediumship: A new resurgence? 179
Reading Auras 182
Trance Mediumship 185
Apports and Asports 187
Traveling Clairvoyance 189
Arriving in the Spirit World 191
Connecting from the Spirit World 193
What is Spiritual Healing? 195
Recommended Reading i

Dedication

I would like to dedicate this book to my parents. They never made me feel uneasy or uncomfortable after I had a near death experience at the age of five. From that day forward, I could sense the Spirit World around me. They always told me to reach for the stars because anything is possible.

I would also like to dedicate this book to my teacher Reverend Leonard Young. He introduced me to this wonderful world of Spiritualism. He taught me and showed me things I could never have imagined. Because of his guidance and encouragement, I was able to write this book and share my thoughts about the religion of Spiritualism and the many great Spiritualists who have gone before me.

"I have found Spiritualism a good thing to live by, and I have come pretty close to finding it a good thing to die by."

Mary S. Vanderbilt

Foreword

To write a forward for any book might be considered a daunting prospect, or even a challenge. However, this is neither. If anything, it is a delight to be writing this forward for such a wonderfully talented and gifted Minister and Medium as Karen.

Karen is a lady full of knowledge, which out surpasses those who profess to know, lecture and teach such a subject as Spiritualism when one finds, in reality, they, in fact, comprehend little of the complexity of such a philosophy. My teacher Ron Baker often said, "A little knowledge is a dangerous thing". A quote which I am sure most of you are well acquainted. It is such a true saying, and yet this cannot be said of Karen Heasley. Karen is a very knowledgeable, and capable lady who possesses an adroit intellect and spiritual awareness that is second to none. Karen's persistent and arduous pursuit of knowledge is clear for all to see within the pages of this book.

I had the privilege of teaching Karen for a considerable number of years in Lily Dale, and at the school, I founded in New Jersey. There is no doubt that Karen has put to good use what she learnt during those years. Karen is a competent Minister, and Medium who is full of compassion, and whose unique desire to serve others is drawn from the very essence of her spiritualistic values which have formed her character, religious awareness and views. She is a true Spiritualist.

Karen has a selfless and compassionate drive to demonstrate the love of the spiritual world through providing a wonderful platform in her church, which she built up herself, for the good of her community and those who seek the comfort of an honest individual whose integrity comes first.

I recommend the pages of this book because it is intelligently written and based on knowledge and facts; something which

Karen has gained through dedication, study and time. Her desire to share this knowledge is a credit to her selfless Ministry, and services to others. Treasure what is written on these pages because they are dedicated to the love of God, and the Spirit World which she serves so well.

The Reverend Leonard Young
Former Vice President and Minister of the Spiritualists' National Union and former course organizer and lecturer at the Arthur Findlay College.

Introduction

Reverend Karen Heasley is a native of New Castle, Pennsylvania. Her journey along the spiritual path began when she had a near death experience at the age of five, dying on an operating table. From that time onward, she has been conscious of the Spirit World. It was almost two decades before she realized that she wasn't the only one who had died and returned to their body. In college, she was introduced to Raymond Moody's book, *Life After Life*. It was a life changing moment for her, but the pressure to "be normal" prevented her from developing her talent.

Karen was employed as a social worker for decades. It wasn't until both of her parents had passed on to the other side, that she was compelled to develop her mediumship skills. She learned platform mediumship from Reverend Leonard Young, who taught at the Arthur Findley College in Stansted, England. She also studied with Reverend Janet Nohavec, from The Journey Within School for Mediumship in New Jersey and several British mediums to improve her evidential mediumship skills.

Karen founded the Spiritual Path Spiritualist Church in New Castle, Pennsylvania in 2008. The church is affiliated with the Spiritualists' National Union (SNU), based in the United Kingdom. Hers is only the third church in the United States under the guidance of the SNU.

Spiritualism does not dictate what to believe or how to interpret religious philosophy, there are no books or preachers whose word must be obeyed. The philosophy of the SNU's Spiritualism is founded upon Seven Fundamental Principles and Spiritualists can interpret them as they think best.

1. The Fatherhood of God
2. The Brotherhood of Man

3. Communion of Spirits and the Ministry of Angels
4. Continuous Existence of the Human Soul
5. Personal Responsibility
6. Compensation and Retribution hereafter for all Good and Evil Deeds done on Earth
7. Eternal Progress open to every Human Soul

Karen is also a member of the Lily Dale Assembly and the International Association for Near-Death Studies, Inc. (IANDS). She founded the Western Pennsylvania IANDS in August 2009 and is available as a resource for those who have had a near-death experience and don't understand what has happened to them.

As part of her goal to educate the public around the world about Spiritualism, she publishes weekly blogs, produces podcasts, and broadcasts a monthly radio show, Truth Seekers on BlogTalk Radio. This book is a compellation of the blogs that have appeared on the church's website.

Section I:

THE RELIGION OF SPIRITUALISM

What Spiritualism is and is Not.

To define Spiritualism, one must look back to one of its early proponents, Emma Hardinge Britten. Britten was born in England in 1823 and was an influential leader in establishing early Spiritualism. She was a passionate orator and writer in the spiritualism movement, as well as a practitioner. She published two significant books, Modern American Spiritualism (1870) and Nineteenth Century Miracles (1884), which are detailed accounts of the early history of the modern spiritualism movement in America.

According to Britten, Spiritualism is "the discovery of a mode whereby discarnate spirits can and do communicate systematically with earth."

Spiritualism teaches that people are, first and foremost, spirits. The body is a material vessel in which the spirt grows and becomes an individual. Once the body dies, the spirit continues eternally.

Communication is the foundation of Spiritualism. Spiritualists are not satisfied to rely on faith alone, as with many other religions. The medium's goal is to demonstrate the existence of a Spirit World by contacting those who have passed from the earthly realm. This doesn't mean bringing forth an intelligence; it means identifying the person who has passed and determining that the communicants are the spirits of the men, women and children who once lived on earth and are now in the Spirit World.

Over the decades, millions of spirits have been reached by mediums. Their names, ages, dates of birth, important events and secrets have been revealed to loved ones. They have communicated by rapping, appearing in photographs, creating paintings, and writing out their desires. They have also directed and inspired healers. Britten said, "they have presented wise and wonderful visions, and in thousands of ways blessed, benefited, and assisted the friends they have left behind."

Although Spiritualism is a means of communication, it does not originate as an earth-based theory or opinion. Mediums relate what they see; none of their authority comes from books written by humans. Spiritualism is not a religion per se, in that it does not need endorsement from any fixed creed, sect or society. Instead, it requires belief through demonstration, as opposed to blind faith. It may be in harmony with some established religions and even the laws of science, but functions independently from them.

According to Britten, Spiritualism proceeds "by virtue of spiritual laws, absolute and true, whether man understands them or not."

Additional Reading:

http://www.ehbritten.org

http://www.bbc.co.uk/religion/religions/spiritualism/

https://www.smithsonianmag.com/history/the-fox-sisters-and-the-rap-on-spiritualism-99663697/

Affiliation Should Not Divide Us

My first experience with the Spirit World occurred when I died on the operating table as a small child. At the time, I knew nothing about Spiritualism, its history or the organizations that existed. The Spirit World accepted me for who I was. Affiliation didn't matter. It wasn't until I was an adult and took my first class, Demonstration of Mediumship with Reverend Leonard Young from England, that I discovered Spiritualism was a religion. I thought wow! A religion that promoted talking to the Spirit World was the perfect fit for me.

After class, Reverend Young introduced his students to Lily Dale, NY. Lily Dale was magical to me. I was a kid in a candy store, meeting like-minded people. At that time, I didn't really understand the organizational structure of different Spiritualist groups. I thought a Spiritualist was a Spiritualist.

When I studied mediumship at Reverend Janet Nohavec's Journey Within Spiritualist Church, Pompton Lakes, NJ, I only knew about the Spiritualists National Union (SNU). It wasn't until I got more familiar with Lily Dale that I learned about the National Spiritualist Association of Churches (NSAC). Later, I attended a worldwide conference in Rochester, NY hosted by the International Spiritualist Federation (ISF).

It didn't matter to me which organization sponsored an event. I was happy just to be around so many Spiritualists who felt the way I did. I will always remember my first Physical Mediumship class with Bill Parkins and the amazing things I learned in his class. All the students had a common bond. We taught each other. One of my classmates even invited me to do a mediumship demonstration at her church. The memory still brings a smile to my face. We were all doing something we loved, serving the Spirit World.

Some may believe that one Spiritualist organization is better than another, but are we so different? The SNU believes the difference between Spiritualism and other religions is the acceptance of mediumship to offer evidence of spirit communication and demonstrate that people survive physical death. The NSAC believes that Spiritualism is the "Science, Philosophy, and Religion of continuous life, based upon the demonstrated fact of communication, by means of mediumship, with those who live in the Spirit World." The ISF was founded on the belief that people survive bodily death and there is communion between this world and the Spirit World. There are also independent Spiritualist churches who believe that there is life after death and we prove it through Mediumship.

It is obvious that, despite our small differences, all Spiritualist organizations have the same beliefs. We are a small group compared to other religions, so we need to stand together, help each other, and spread Spiritualism wherever we go. My church members and I participated in the 2014 World Congress of Spiritualists at Lily Dale. Our interaction with Spiritualists from around the world showed me how united we can be.

Additional Reading:

https://www.snu.org.uk/

http://nsac.org/

https://www.theisf.com/

The Spirit World: All Around Us

Many of us think of the Spirit World as being—OUT THERE. It sits apart from the earth. It could be a heaven above, or an overlapping dimension, a place of oneness with God or a place of waiting.

In the Bible, St. Paul mentioned the third level of heaven. By the Middle Ages, Dante's poem, Divine Comedy, took readers through nine spiritual levels, including purgatory and hell. Latter-day Saints doctrine states that the Spirit World is a place where spirits wait for the resurrection. Disembodied spirits live in different conditions according to their mortal lives. Hindi followers believe the soul is reincarnated until it achieves perfection and reaches the otherworld where the soul exists in peace. Buddha focused on teaching how to attain a high level of consciousness or nirvana rather than an afterlife.

Some modern spiritualists believe the Spirit World consists of seven concentric spheres around our planet, with the first sphere being a buffer zone between the physical and spiritual planes. Others think there are times, such as sunrise and sunset when the "veil" is thin between worlds.

Emanuel Swedenborg was a Swedish scientist, mathematician and inventor who lived in the early 1700s. He began to experience dreams and visions in 1744 which resulted in a spiritual awakening and lead to the publication, *The Heavenly Doctrine*, his attempt to reform Christianity. Swedenborg referred to hell as a "place, as well as a condition." His writings influenced Spiritualist, Andrew Jackson Davis, 100 years later. But Davis saw things differently.

Davis did not experience the Spirit World as a place with complicated levels. According to him, the Spirit World existed right here. "And, lo!" he said. "here I am in the Spirit World. Yet I have not moved an inch into space. In the Spirit World, I behold the interior of the Natural World...I suddenly see a beautiful assemblage which seems far away, and yet I inwardly know that the association is within the gravitation of the earth, or rather, Spirit World."

As a Medium, my contact with spirits has given me insights into the Spirit World. Like Davis, I do not feel the Spirit World is a location based outside the world. There is no heaven above or hell below. There are no levels of heaven. When I contact the spirits, I do so by raising my vibrations. At the same time, the spirits must lower their vibrations to reach me. They are reaching me not from another location, but from another vibration.

Additional Reading:

Davis, Andrew Jackson, "Where is the Spirit World – We are in it!" The Pioneer, Vol. 3, No. 5, October 2016. Page 180

http://www.ascsi.org/ASCS/Library/LegacyRoom/Biographies/Davis_AJ.pdf

https://swedenborg.com/

Spheres of the Spirit World

James Hewat McKenzie was born in 1869 in Edinburgh, Scotland. By 1900, he had left his practice as a psychologist and psychoanalyst to pursue parapsychology full-time. He wrote his seminal work, *Spirit Intercourse: Its Theory and Practice* in 1917. He also helped a number of spiritualist mediums develop their abilities, including: Gladys Osborne Leonard, Franek Kluski, Maria Silbert and Eileen J. Garrett. He founded the British College of Psychic Science with his wife in 1920 and died in 1929. McKenzie's research contributed to the spiritual movement of the early 20th century, paving the way for future study of clairvoyance, extrasensory perception and remote viewing.

The Spirit World has been described as an ethereal plane that exists in the same space as the earth, but descriptions differ considerably from one medium to the next. In his book, McKenzie described the Spirit World as he envisioned it, and went on to explain why he thought there were contradicting descriptions.

McKenzie describe the Spirit World as a set of seven spheres that surrounded each planet in the solar system. "The sun would not be seen as a physical object upon the seventh or any other super-physical sphere, for it illuminates physical matter only," he wrote. There was no heaven and hell. "The old idea of heaven was a dead level of experience for the 'good' and another level for the 'bad,' but the new conception pictures all, at various stages of progress, mostly happy and contented, and never left without help and instruction when they desire these at any stage."

The first and second spheres were described as basic levels, very similar to earth. The third sphere, located 1,350 miles from the earth's surface, was a transitional point that had pets, animals, gardens, houses, plants, flowers and trees. The forth level was the Philosopher's Sphere. Located 2,850 miles above the surface, it held some plants and animals, but inhabitants lived together in brotherhoods, "devoting much their time to intellectual, artistic and ascetic pursuits." The fifth sphere had fewer animals and plants and was devoted to contemplation, aspiration and helping others. The sixth level he called the Love Sphere. Highly evolved birds and flowers were some of the few reminders with the physical world. The seventh sphere he called the Christ Sphere. Located 18,250 miles above the surface, it was no longer composed of earth, but was crystalline in nature. This sphere was filled with dazzling brightness, streets of gold and buildings of jasper.

He explained the contradictions coming from spirits through their mediums as one of viewpoint. The spirit's view of the world is dependent upon which level he resides. "One who enters the astral plane after death will describe life there," he wrote. "Quite ignorant of higher states, while those who enter directly into the third sphere will be similarly unable to tell what the life of a spirit is upon the astral plane."

When re-counting time and space, he said that space exists, but "time is difficult to reckon in spirit life, as it is of little importance in comparison with development, for a spirit is only judged to have wasted time if he has not evolved."

He described the transition from sphere to sphere. "Man has a soul composed of several envelopes or bodies. The grossest is the astral which he uses to enter the astral world, in the first sphere." The Spirit World acts as a purifier on the astral body, "reducing its density atom by atom like chemical evaporation."

He stated that, "Man's idea of physical and spiritual states is delusive. It is purely a matter of standpoint as to how these seemingly contrary states shall be judged. For the spiritual world is just as concrete a reality to spirits as the physical earth is a reality to mortals."

Additional Reading:

https://www.scribd.com/document/82168750/Spirit-Intercourse-j-Hewat-Mckenzie

The Titanic Sinking from the Other Side

While Estelle Stead's father, William T. Stead, was on the Titanic bound for America, Estelle was traveling with a Shakespearean Acting Company. She didn't worry about her father being on the long journey. Titanic was supposed to be the greatest ship ever built.

On the very day that the Titanic sank, Estelle was having tea with another member of the acting company, Pardoe Woodman. Pardoe was a gifted psychic, and without her prompting, brought up a vision he had experienced. He told her he'd seen a disaster at sea and that an elderly man connected to her would perish.

Of course, we all know about the Titanic today. Estelle's father was one of over 1,500 souls who died in the cold sea. Two weeks after the disaster, Estelle visited Etta Wreidt, a direct voice medium from the United States. Estelle quickly recognized her father's voice and spoke with him for about twenty minutes.

By 1917, Pardoe Woodman had learned automatic writing, and Estelle communicated with her father that way. She said she could sometimes see light surrounding them in the room, and other times see the figure of her father during their weekly sessions.

In 1922, her father began dictating information about the Spirit World. It was published in the book, *The Blue Island*. One interesting aspect of the book is William Stead's description of the spirits passing on to the Spirit World from the Titanic.

In the forward of the book, William dictated, "In earth life I did my best to help and enlighten, but I was very restricted owing to material calls upon my time. Since my arrival in this land I have tried to carry on and greatly increase the amount and the sphere of this same work."

In the book's first chapter, William said that what he learned on the earthly plan helped him to understand and recognize what was happening in the Spirit World. He was uplifted by the fact that he could lend a hand to others. That was not the case for many who perished on the Titanic.

William said that during the disaster, spirits waited until the saved were saved and "the dead—alive." The spirit group then moved from the scene together. "It was a strange method of travelling for us all, and we were a strange crew, bound for we knew not where."

He described the hundreds of bodies floating in the water and the hundreds of souls floating in the air. Many realized that they had died and were angry that they couldn't save their valuables. He found it "both heartbreaking and repellant."

Once they were all collected, he said they "seemed to rise vertically into the air at a terrific speed." He didn't know how long the journey lasted, but when they arrived at the place, they saw it was bright and beautiful. They were greeted by old friends and relatives and were free to part company from the other survivors.

"I will not say that none were unhappy" he said. "Many were, but that was because they did not understand the nearness of the two worlds; they did not know what was possible..." To William, this was just the beginning of a fascinating new journey.

Additional Reading:

Woodman, Pardoe and Estelle Stead (1922) *The Blue Island: experiences of a new arrival beyond the veil.* Hutchinson & Co., London.

Available at: https://archive.org/details/blueislandexperioostea

Passing Over to the Other Side

As a minister of a Spiritualist church, I find that the passing of a loved one is the most difficult time for a family. I had a Near Death Experience as a child, so I have already taken a step into the other side. But how do I help families deal with their grief?

One of the greatest gifts a Spiritualist can give to a family is to help them understand the transition that their loved one experiences during passing. The person has finished their physical journey here on earth and is now moving on to their spiritual journey. My job as a Spiritualist is to be at the person's bedside during their passing to make them comfortable and help them make the transition. My assistance is not only for the person who is passing, it involves the entire family.

Different things occur when a person is passing. They may say see loved ones who gone on before. They may see strangers who are there to assist them. They may ask if they are hallucinating. I am there to reassure them and inform them that what they are seeing is real.

I was only five years old when I traveled to the other side. As a child, I experienced the event with the understanding of a child. Because of that, I like to read about the Near-Death Experiences of others to have a greater understanding of the process.

One of those people is Emanuel Swedenborg, a Swedish scientist, philosopher, theologian and mystic who lived in the late 1600s. Swedenborg referred to the passing of the spirit as the awakening. He said, "I have not only been told how the awakening happens, I have been shown by firsthand experience. The actual experience happened to me so that I could have a full knowledge of how it occurs."

He explained the process of transitioning to the other side. "We are only separated from the physical nature that was useful to us in the world. The essential person is actually still alive. I say that the essential person is still alive because we are not people because of our bodies but because of our spirits." He saw death as resurrection or a continuance of life.

Swedenborg said that he was first contacted by angels. They sat near his head, silent, sharing their thoughts with him in a telepathic way. They kept watch over him, waiting for his body to breathe its last breath. "When heavenly angels are with people who have been awakened, they do not leave them, because they love everyone." At the same time, he felt a tug, like his spirit was being pulled from his body.

He spoke about angels rolling back a covering from his left eye toward the center of his nose so that he could see. "I could see a kind of clear but dim light like the light we see through our eyelids when we are first waking up. It seemed to me as though this clear, dim light had a heavenly color to it," he said. After that, something was rolled back from his face.

According to Swedenborg, angels do everything for newly arrived spirits. They inform them, at least to the extent that they can grasp, about the realities of their new life. If newly arrived spirits do not want to be taught, they are free to move on. Other good spirits accompany them and do all they can for them. If the departed was not a good person in the physical world and wants to get away from these good intentioned spirits as well, they are free to go. They may search until they find the company of people more attuned to their own spiritual development. Swedenborg explained that some spirits "remarkable as it may sound, then lead the same kind of life they had led in the world."

According to Swedenborg, the first stage of our life on the other side does not last more than a few days. After that, the spirit travels from one state into another until finally it arrives either in heaven or in hell.

Additional Reading:

Swedenborg, Emanuel & Donald L. Rose, Afterlife: A Guided Tour of Heaven and Its Wonders, Second Edition. iBooks.

Spirit Guides Part I: Silver Birch

The third principle of Spiritualism is: The Communion of Spirits and the Ministry of Angels. The Ministry of Angels is said to bring enhanced wisdom to enlighten the individual, as well as the society and world in which we live.

Spirit guides are some of the angels that contact us through mediums. Because their instruction can be enlightening, I want to take some time to discuss some of the more noteworthy spirit guides of the past.

Silver Birch was a spirit guide who spoke through Maurice Barbanell (1902-1981). Barbanell was the founder and editor of the Psychic News of London. Silver Birch's teachings became popular in the late 1930s and resulted in the publication of nine books documenting his communications.

Silver Birch took on the identity of a Native American and he said he was only acting as translator. "I am but a humble servant," he said. "an interpreter for those who have sent me to expound forgotten laws that must be revived as part of the new world that is gradually dawning. Think of me always as a mouthpiece. I represent the voice of the spirit that seeks to make its presence felt in your world and which is succeeding in increasing measure." His described a group of communicators who harmonized their minds to create the messages that he gave to Barbanell.

Silver Birch gave few details about his own earthy existence but mentioned that his last lifetime occurred about 3,000 years earlier. While on earth, he said he worshiped many gods, but had learned in the Spirit World that "there is only one Great Spirit, who has provided eternal laws for the control of every phase of life throughout the boundless universe."

Barbanell's book, Thou Shall Be Comforted, discusses Silver Birch's teachings on existence after physical death. When we pass on, he said that we do not enter Heaven through "pearly gates", neither do we descend to Hell through lakes of "fire and brimstone." The person who has died will be the same individual as they were in life, except that they will have no physical body. The spirit body is a replica of the physical one, but without any of its physical imperfections.

Silver Birch made it clear that the Spirit World is not "dreamy or nebulous." Spirits are busy with activities just as they are in the physical world. In the Spirit World, the mental is real and the physical is a shadow. For example, when one dreams, things seem real at the time. The dream only becomes ethereal when the person wakes up. It's the viewpoint that makes the difference. He also said that the Spirit World isn't a separate place. It is all around us, blending and intermingling with the physical world.

When one arrives in the Spirit World, the person meets those who have preceded him. Families and friends are reunited most of the time, but because of the law of attraction, only those of similar spiritual qualities will meet on the same plane. Married couples or family members who held no real love for each other will not be together in the Spirit World.

The Spirit World may take on the trappings of physical existence, including homes, clothing and food. Silver Birch said this was a habit from our physical make-up. The houses are not made of bricks and mortar but constructed out of thought. Desire for food is a mental craving and a spirit can maintain the illusion if it requires it. People are free to express their talents, with no physical limitations. People also speak the same language -- thought. Those thoughts are never hidden and lying is impossible.

After a person passes into the Spirit World, he naturally gravitates to the spiritual sphere or vibration according to the life lived and the character evolved on the earthly plane. A person cannot occupy a higher sphere than the spiritual status he has reached, but spirits can evolve over time to reach higher spheres.

Additional Reading:

Barbanell, Maurice (1936). *They Shall Be Comforted*. Psychic Press, Ltd.

Spirit Guides Part II: Choo Chow

Gordon Higginson trained from a very early age to be a platform medium and began working in public at the age of twelve. He was known for the accuracy of his platform mediumship which often included full names, addresses and telephone numbers. He demonstrated at many of the largest venues in the England and left behind many recordings.

As a trance medium, Higginson had several spiritual guides. His childhood friend, Cuckoo, and Irish guide, Paddy, were humorous. The guide named Light only appeared once a year, usually during Christmas. His main guide, Choo Chow, visited often and provided spiritual words of wisdom.

During a 1988 trance, Choo Chow was recorded speaking through Higginson during an address. He began with a blessing from the Spirit World and said there was a host of souls gathered there. "Those who are your family, your friends and those who have been drawn to you from our world because of the great bond of love between sides."

Choo Chow stressed that unity between the earthly plane and spiritual word was important. "Put aside the things that may come between us," he said. "As we gain life from the same father, we are one. We have the same opportunities and destinies." He said that if we accept help from the Spirit World, we will be filled with the great power that links souls together. "You will be filled to overflowing with the power of pure life."

Choo Chow stated that the "great mind" or "creative force" had set things in motion so that we could experience the earthy plane for ourselves. But each of us has a responsibility while we are here. "You must play your part," he said. He spoke of uniting the nations of the world. He said there would be "many hardships and pain to bear and times of uncertainty will smother the earth." Our job will be to unite, not divide.

Choo Chow explained that the great minds of earth were linked with the great minds of the Spirit World. He asked all of us to "seek deep for the heaven within you." He also said that young souls were waiting to come to earth. It was our responsibility to ready things for them, so they could begin change when they arrived.

"There is love for you," Choo Chow said. "We met in this way this time, but we have met many times before." He stressed that he was there to bring a message of hope, "a sea of hope." He said we must find the power in our own being and let wisdom be our guide.

He wanted us all to understand: "I come to you with a message of love, not for you to be afraid, but to know."

Additional Reading

Recordings of Trance and Physical Mediumship can be found at: http://www.gordonhigginson.co.uk/trance-and-physical/4575482114

Spirit Guides Part III: Maurice de la Tour

Coral Polge was born in London in 1924. Most mediums communicate with the Spirit World through thought messages, but Coral combined her artistic talent and psychic gift into a technique that reached the Spirit World through drawings.

Coral began her journey as a psychic artist while meeting with a small group of individuals who were trying to improve their psychic talents. She worked with several spirit artists who helped her improve her skills until she became one of the most renown psychic artists of her time.

One of her guides was a spirit named Giovanni Masaccio who said he was from Italy. After some research, Coral found a Tommaso (another version of Masaccio) from San Giovanni who had lived in Italy in the early 1400s. Masaccio was one of several guides who returned over the years to help guide Coral's hand. "In the early days," she said. "there was a concentration on teaching me to use pastels and coaching me in anatomy and the guides were endeavoring to balance three aspects—the artistic or material channel, the psychic, and the spiritual."

Her most helpful spirit guide was a French pastel artist named Maurice de la Tour. He first appeared in the 1960s and called himself only Maurice. He didn't help Coral at first, but was identified by other mediums as a Frenchman, dressed in 18th century clothing with lace ruffles, and wearing a wig. Coral managed to make a sketch of him, but she wouldn't know who Maurice was until later.

During a reading, Maurice communicated with Coral's husband, telling her husband more about his life and that he had been helping Coral with her artistry. Coral accidentally came across a book with the self-portrait of a French artist. She discovered his name was Maurice de la Tour. When they found Maurice's autobiography, many of the facts he had given her husband were confirmed.

Maurice is a stickler when it comes to Coral's work. In her book, *Living Images*, Coral says, "Even now, Maurice de la Tour shows a great sense of frustration when I am unable to produce the quality of line or colour he has in mind."

Additional Reading:

Polge, Coral and Kay Hunter. (1997). *Living Images: The Story of a Psychic Artist*. Spiritualist Association of Great Britain.

Spirit Guides Part IV: Light

Gordon Higginson trained from a very early age to be a platform medium and began working in public at the age of twelve. Because of his accuracy, he became well-known, demonstrated at many of the largest venues in the England, and left behind many recordings. As a trance medium, Higginson had several spiritual guides. Light only appeared once a year during Christmas and would give a prophesy for the coming year.

Light's last appearance was on Christmas Day of 1992, less than a month before Higginson died. The spirit spoke of the end of Higginson's ministry, but also had other messages that are still relevant today. I will let the spirit speak for itself. Below is an excerpt from Light's Christmas message:

"New thoughts and ideas face the world. Channels of the Spirit will be made again. We come with the message of Love Divine. For change is here upon the Earth. Throughout the world, the cry for peace is heard by the wise ones of our world.

"And so they are born, who are to serve. And among you here are those who have been touched by the Great Spirit. You are called to give, that the world may receive. You are called to build. You are called to sow the seeds of love. But you will not reap the harvest, for the harvest is meant for those who yet are to be born to the Earth. We come because the message of hope is the message that the world needs. The message to bring mankind together.

"And so the world is facing change. Change that some want, and some do not and yet the fight must go on. Great souls are coming to the Earth. Great powers are being gifted to those who are chosen. Once again, you will hear of the great miracles of the past being shown to mankind in these days. For materialism is coming to an end and the great battle of Spirit is beginning to show its head of victory.

"Great souls have come to the earth, waiting for the opportunity to be able to bring their message of goodwill. And across the world, in every country of the world, will rise the mighty Spirit. For there will be those that will speak with great tongues of wisdom, and bringing forth the great light, which will shine in the darkened places of the world.

"But yet there are those unhappy periods still to take place. There are still those who will want to bring battle and bring horror to the earth. There are still those that are waiting to grasp the power of nations. You have passed through the foundation for a new world. All the horrific experiences are the battle of the forces against each other. And before the world can rise triumphantly in love, then hatred and jealousy and all the horrific things of the world must die. The great powers of our world are waiting. Waiting for you. Waiting for your hearts to open and your souls to express the Divine that is within you.

"So this Christmas morning, the Angel world, so close to your Earth, brings with it the powers of the great wise ones of the past. Then this earth will blossom again. All the gladness and all the spiritual freedom that has been won through the sacrifices of those of the past will come like the dawn of the day. Across the horizons will come the light which will come from the world of the Spirit. We reach you this morning to tell you that, although you will face hardship, yet there will come the clouds will fall away, because the light of the Spirit will shine through them. We reach you with the power to tell you, to strengthen your hearts, with that which shall take you forward. And let your hearts be brave and face the many tomorrows. The world needs the power that comes from your soul. The world needs the great minds of the Spirit to be able to co-operate with the thoughts of those who lead the nations of the world."

Additional Reading:

Higginson, Gordon. (1993) On the Side of Angels: Authorized Life Story. Tudor Press.

The remainder of the message can be found at:

http://www.gordonhigginson.co.uk/light-address/4558861171

Spirit Guides Part V: Red Cloud

Estelle Roberts was born in May 1889 in Kensington, a suburb of London. She was married three times and had a total of 4 children. Her third husband, Charles Tilson-Chrowne, was a Spiritualist who worked alongside her as a healer, but he too passed-over like her previous husbands.

As a child, Estelle encountered spirits, but she didn't develop as a medium until she was in her thirties. She conducted many séances and demonstrated using several forms of mediumship, including physical materialization and direct voice. In the 1950's she was instrumental in obtaining the legal recognition of Spiritualism by the British Government.

As a trance medium, she connected with her spirit guide, Red Cloud. "I've worked with Red Cloud for nearly fifteen years, and during that time he has toiled unceasingly to demonstrate eternal spirit truth. He has never told us who he was on earth. When asked, he has always answered: 'Know me by my works.' We know that he passed this way before us, when he probably dwelt in Egypt. We believe, too, that he was either in this world, or very near to it, in the days of Jesus of Nazareth," she said of her guide.

Red Cloud spoke on a variety of topics, all of which have been published by SDU Publications. One of the topics is "Where is Spiritualism Leading You?" He begins to answer this question by equating Spiritualism with the Christianity of two-thousand years ago, and the natural law of four-thousand years ago. He rephrased the question to, "Where is the great truth leading you?"

The first thing he emphasized was that we all have freewill to think for ourselves. "You, and you alone, will reap what you sow.

Whether good or bad, it is for you to decide." He added that we can say all the prayers we want, but none of those prayers will help us if we don't help ourselves. He said the Bible can be a resource, but "read the Bible for yourselves, not through another man's mind, not even through mine."

Red Cloud said a great truth leads us, and like St. Paul said in Corinthians, if "there be none risen from the dead 'then all my teaching is in vain.' If there be none risen from the dead all of our teaching is in vain." He said the world needs to awaken to accept both freewill and personal responsibility.

Unification of all religious and spiritual beliefs and peoples is necessary for progress. "One of the things I find as I look around your earth world—I am sorry to say this—is that the brotherhood of man is practiced more by those who have no dogmas and creeds."

He added that we must understand the law of cause and effect and that materialism is destroying spiritual truth. "Spiritualism can teach man how to put his own world right, adjust his own laws, appeal to his God for sustenance." He said the job of the spirit guide was to show people how to live in the world and manifest universal love.

"Once you begin to awaken to your responsibilities," he said. "the veil will be stripped away, and you will see God in humanity."

Additional Reading:

Fifty Years a Medium, Estelle Roberts at:

https://archive.org/stream/FIFTYYEARSAMEDIUMbyEstelleRoberts/FIFTYYEARSAMEDIUMbyEstelleRoberts_djvu.txt

Roberts, Estelle (2013) Red Cloud Speaks, Estelle Roberts, SDU Publications, Croydon, UK

The Ministry of Angels

The other day I was watching the movie, *It's a Wonderful Life*, during which an angel helps a distraught businessman by showing him what life would be like if he never existed. I assume most people identify with Jimmy Stewart's character, George Bailey. But the character I love the most is Bailey's guardian angel, Clarence, played by Henry Travers.

Most people probably imagine guardian angels as perfect beings with flawless dispositions clad in white robes, halos and wings. Clarence is a kindly, unassuming soul. After he saves George from an intended suicide, we find that he is not a perfect being. He has come to earth to earn his wings. To do that he must help George.

It's been said that angels are the most under-employed souls because people here on this earthly plane never ask for their help. It is no coincidence that Spiritualists believe in the Ministry of Angels. We believe that angels never existed on Earth in physical form but are immortal beings who take on the role of God's divine helpers. It is through them that He makes known His purpose and will. Angels serve God and act on His authority for the good of His other creations. Their role is to show us our spiritual path and awaken an awareness of God's plan within us.

Most of us are familiar with the notion of guardian angels. These are angels who take on the special responsibility of helping us discover our true purpose here on Earth. Guardian angels come close to us when we are in trouble or need. They assist us by offering protection and support and easing our fears in times of distress. "They bring the light of eternal truth for our upliftment and they rejoice when we are happy and fulfilled," Carol Austin wrote.

We can ask angels for help, but it must be understood, that they will not interfere with our responsibility to conduct our lives in accordance with our own conscience. That responsibility is ours alone to bear. "We know that with the guidance of compassionate spiritual and angelic beings we shall move towards fulfilment of the purpose for which our earthly lives were intended," Austin wrote.

I love our Christmas Eve service at the Spiritual Path Church because every year we meditate to open ourselves to the angels. This is something many people have never done before, and our service is open to the community. The practice helps people become aware of their guardian angels. Two members of my church were asked about their experiences.

"It was a time of my life when I needed to feel more grounded in my spiritual practice," Ruth Kovac said. "and I 'happened' to see an angel meditation being offered at a local church. My friend and I went, and I found it a peaceful place to be, and found a peaceful place inside myself. I am grateful for that and for the community that I found."

"One present I give myself each Christmas Eve is attending a candlelight service called, Sitting in the Power of the Angels," Gerri Heckler added. "Too much jingling, shopping and parties can easily pull me away from how I like to feel during this season. Soft candlelight and soothing music quiets my mind and connects me with God and His glorious angels who quickly restore my soul with joy, peace, hope and love--the perfect gifts to share with others."

During the movie, it's mentioned that every time you hear a bell ring an angel has gotten its wings. The Third Principle of Spiritualism maintains the human experience of linking with individual spirits and higher beings and affirms that we can both commune and communicate with them. It is my fervent wish and hope for everyone is that you too will find your own Clarence this holiday season.

Additional Reading:

Austin, Carole: David Hopkins & Barry Oates (2013) *The Philosophy of Spiritualism*. The Spiritualists' National Union, iBooks.

Personal Responsibility

A Christmas Carol by Charles Dickens made its debut in 1843. It was the most successful book of the Christmas holiday season. Eight plays were produced within a few months of the book's publication. By 1908, one of the earliest films based on the book opened, and dozens of adaptations have been filmed since then. It is not surprising that the story has maintained its popularity for over 150 years. It is a straightforward narrative filled with symbolic meaning and spiritual lessons.

Ebenezer Scrooge, with his "Bah Humbug" attitude, is a man of greed, selfishness, and lack of consideration for his fellow man. One night he is visited by three spirit guides. The Ghost of Christmas Past comes to him as a representative of the truth and reveals that Scrooge's past Christmases were filled with loneliness. The Ghost of Christmas Present symbolizes all the joy and generosity of Christmas, evident by the mound of food and the torch which bestows blessings upon poor. The Ghost of Christmases Yet to Come takes Scrooge to his grave. His gravestone is emblematic of his heartless and miserly ways. The grave is neglected because Scrooge didn't foster good relationships when he has alive.

In the first section of the book, Scrooge's deceased partner, Jacob Marley, appears to him in chains. Marley tells Scrooge that he made the chain around his neck by being selfish and greedy throughout his life. "I made it link by link, and yard by yard," he said. Dickens uses chains as a warning to Scrooge and the reader that one cannot escape the consequences of such behavior.

It is no coincidence that Personal Responsibility is one of the Laws governing Spiritualism. We have been given enormous potential to improve our own lives and the lives of others. We are free to make decisions throughout our lives as we see fit. What each of us makes of our life is our own Personal Responsibility, and no one can replace or override that right. At the same time, no other person or influence can right our errors. We must do that ourselves.

When Dickens wrote the book, Scrooge signified Victorian aristocracy who viewed the poor as a scourge upon the earth. The story was about the plight of the poor and the dangers of social neglect. By creating the Cratchit family, he reminded his readers to be inclusive as a society and to care for those who need help. It is apparent that poverty still exists in the 21st Century, and like Scrooge, we can choose to help those in need or not.

Another Law of Spiritualism is the Compensation and Retribution Hereafter for all the Good and Evil Deeds done on Earth. This law operates on earth as well as in the Spirit World. As we make life choices, the outcome of those choices affects our soul's growth. When we leave this earthly life, there will be no divine judgement. We will have the opportunity to reassess, take stock and decide what might have been done differently.

In Dickens' story, Scrooge is given the opportunity to reassess his life before passing from the earthly plane. He sees how self-serving and insensitive he had been. He is converted into a charitable, caring, and socially conscious member of society through the intercession of the Christmas spirits. Warmth, generosity, and overall goodwill overcome his bitter apathy. Empathy enables him to sympathize with and understand those less fortunate than himself, like Tiny Tim and Bob Cratchit.

During the Christmas season, we too can reassess our lives. That could mean helping the poor, or maybe just shoveling the neighbor's sidewalk. Maybe you have a loved one who is isolated and alone for the holidays. Maybe you have a special gift you can share with others, or just offer someone your company. This is the season, not to wait for Christmas Spirits, but to become one yourself.

A Life of Giving Thanks: Part I

As Thanksgiving approaches, many of us are told to be grateful, but what does Spiritualism teach us?

Spiritualism had traditionally focused on the belief that spirits can communicate with the living through a medium. Emanuel Swedenborg was one of the first to use the term in 1796. He believed that a vital component within living beings was supernatural and divine.

As Spiritualism developed, many believers and mediums concentrated on the communication aspect of the belief. Mediums did not take to the podium to preach morality and religious practices. Instead, they acted as conduits between the spiritual realm to the physical world. Because of this, there are few teachings from them about ways to deal with life.

In Spiritualism, the Seven Principles do include Personal Responsibility. We are to make decisions throughout our lives as we see fit. What each of us makes of our life is our choice. No one can replace or override that right. No other person or influence can correct our wrong doings.

Although not part of Spiritualism doctrine, gratitude can be adopted as part of our responsibility in life.

Swedenborg mentioned in his writings the importance of thanksgiving and gratitude. "The Lord does, indeed, require humility, worship, thanksgiving, and many other things from us," he said. "This might seem like repayment, so that the Lord's gifts do not seem to be free. But the Lord does not require these things for his own sake.... Rather, they are required for our sake. If we are humble, we can accept goodness from the Lord, since we have been separated from selfishness and the evil things that go with it, which stand in the way of our accepting the Lord's goodness. This is why the Lord desires a state of humility in us for our own sake: because when we are in this state, the Lord can flow into us with heavenly goodness. The same is true of worship and thanksgiving."

When we are grateful, we recognize that we are a recipient of many gifts. The most basic gift is life itself. Swedenborg said that the more open our heart is, the fuller of life we are.

It is often easy to be grateful when things are going our way. But what do we do when things get tough? We must still strive to be grateful. An "attitude of gratitude" will make the difference between a life of fulfillment or emptiness. Psychological research is showing that grateful people tend to have higher levels of happiness and lower levels of stress and depression.

Being grateful is more than saying you are thankful. Instead, it is a positive feeling towards someone who has given to you, as well as a desire to do something good in return. I invite you to cultivate gratefulness as your basic attitude toward life. It will make the difference between going through the motions and really being alive.

Additional Reading:

Arcana Coelestia #5957 at https://swedenborg.com/emanuel-swedenborg/writings/

A Life of Giving Thanks: Part II

"He is a wise man who does not grieve for the things which he has not, but rejoices for those which he has"

(Epictetus)

Ancient philosopher, Epictetus, knew that gratitude puts everything into perspective. It enables us to see the blessings around us. The more we give thanks, the more things we find to be grateful for.

Modern science agrees with Epictetus. Studies have revealed that people who write letters of gratitude feel fewer symptoms of depression and feel happier and more satisfied with life overall. People who take time to focus on the positive gestures of their partners are more connected and satisfied in their relationship. People who practice gratitude for twenty-one days or more find their mental health and wellbeing increases. Gratitude also leads to better sleep and more energy.

Of course, gratitude takes practice. For many of us, we must create an attitude of gratitude one day at a time. In this season of thanks and giving, try this twelve-day trial of being grateful to put yourself on a path of thankfulness.

1. **Day 1:** During a meal, be thankful for the food by relishing each bite with all your senses.
2. **Day 2:** To thank a business for their good service, recommend it to your friends.

3. **Day 3:** Appreciate natures gifts by incorporating some of them into your home decor.
4. **Day 4:** Sit with your pets and let them know how grateful you are to have them in your life.
5. **Day 5:** Select something you use every day and acknowledge how it helps you.
6. **Day 6:** Give thanks for peace and all the peacemakers in your life.
7. **Day 7:** Write a letter or email of appreciation to someone who has inspired you.
8. **Day 8:** Express your gratitude to a good friend by giving them a small token.
9. **Day 9:** Donate to a charity with a note of your appreciation.
10. **Day 10:** Do a chore or run an errand for a neighbor.
11. **Day 11:** Thank your spouse or significant other for being in your life.
12. **Day 12:** Give thanks for your good health when you rise in the morning.

A Religion of Self-Mastery

Spiritualism is often lumped together with crystal gazing, astrology, tarot cards and other forms of divination. Psychics and mediums are considered one and the same. One reason for this may be that Spiritualism has no creed except for a set of principles that state accepted truths. There is neither holy book nor great leader to follow. It is a religion of Self-Mastery

Spiritualism is designed to promote the development of the spirit, but people respond to it in many ways.

Some enter into a study of the religion because they are curious. They may approach a medium with a "show me" attitude, expecting the Spirit World to respond immediately to their call. They have yet to realize that the spirits work at their own pace and on their own schedule. The curious don't see that they must develop their own consciousness to be open to communication.

Others approach Spiritualism with a scientific attitude. They want to investigate the phenomena in order to better understand the Spirit World and our connection to it. Their goal is to measure and prove the existence of life after death. But like the curious person, the scientist doesn't understand that he or she must pursue their own development as well.

Many use Spiritualism only to receive messages. They may want to know which path they should follow in their life and expect the medium to instruct them. They might want to speak with a loved one who has passed on. They remain with their own Orthodox religion, and never understand the true goal of Spiritualism.

"Spiritualism is the religion of self-culture, the religion of self-building, the religion of self-attainment, the religion of self-mastery," H. Gordon Burroughs wrote. With self-mastery, each of us can learn to reach a higher state of vibration where we can communicate with the Spirit World. It takes practice and determination and belief.

"Masters are universal," Burroughs wrote. "and come to whoever wills; and whosoever knocks on the door may have it opened to him. The Masters are only waiting until the student has made the approach; and when the student has reached them, they, the Masters of Light, appear to guide the faltering footsteps over the pathway of life."

Spiritualism is more than predicting the future or receiving messages from loved ones; it is a religion of self-development. We are constantly progressing or retrogressing. There is no standing still. With the right guidance, we can view humanity in a new light, we can evolve into people with higher attributes of understanding, sympathy and humility. We can transform ourselves from physical beings into spiritual ones.

Additional Reading:

Burroughs, H. Gordon (1962). *Becoming A Spiritualist.* Port City Press

A Religion of Introspection

Established religions each contain truths and half-truths. They depend upon holy books written centuries ago. Although they offer guidelines for life, each is limited because God is interpreted as being outside of oneself. They separate the person from a spiritual oneness with the infinite intelligence.

For one seeking to live in harmony with life on the earthly plane, religions often erect roadblocks of laws, rites and judgements which impede progress. Spiritualism teaches that each individual must find his or her own way in this life. We are all personally responsible for establishing harmony by obeying infinite laws, not man-made ones.

A follower of Spiritualism finds God by constantly looking within, not without. When we rid ourselves of religious prejudice and dogma, we begin to grow. There may be many obstacles, but if we carefully seek the truth, we will begin to see that emotions like jealousy, hatred, envy, and greed are products of individual selfishness. They must be cast out before we can proceed on the path toward infinite intelligence. When we reach that ideal, we will see the infinite intelligence manifesting everywhere.

Only by looking inward with an open mind will we begin to discover the divine plan of infinite intelligence which governs all things. Only after our own struggle, will we be ready to take on the greater task of helping others on their way through life. As this desire begins to manifest, others who seek the truth will be attracted to you. Hugh Gordon Burroughs was the Vice President of the National Spiritualist Association of Churches and founder of the Church of Two Worlds. Before he passed in 1971, he wrote, "By being of service here on the earth plane, he renders service to infinite intelligence; and in so doing, he achieves greater happiness here as well as hereafter."

Along with helping others discover their own connection with the infinite intelligence, Spiritualism requires that we be receptive to the vibrations that reach us from the greater universe. Through conscious living and openness, you are in the position to receive communications from the Spirit World. "Within every human being is the power of receiving from the great reservoir of infinite intelligence from which can be supplied all human needs. Here all true knowledge is waiting to be drawn upon by every child of this great universe," wrote Burroughs.

Burroughs said the student desiring development should meditate a few minutes each day and repeat the following: "I know that more things are wrought by prayer then this world dreams of; therefore, my voice will rise like a fountain in prayer for myself, for those whom I call friends, and for all mankind. Oh infinite intelligence, ruler of the universe, make me more receptive to thy blessings and to Thee. May I be more conscious of the great knowledge around and about me; and may I, as I grow more able to know Thee, receive bountifully from Thee, that I may impart real knowledge to my fellow man."

By developing your spiritual receptivity, you will reach a greater capacity for joy and a greater capacity to help others. You will begin to arrive.

Additional Reading:

Burroughs, H. Gordon (1962) *Becoming A Spiritualist*, Port City Press.

A Religion of Lifting Self and Others.

H. Gordon Burroughs said, "Spiritualism shows the seeker the way, the open door to attainment." Attainment of what?

Spiritualism teaches that continual change is the only truth in life. Man is constantly progressing or retrogressing. Each of us is born into an ever-changing environment. As children, our bodies grow and age. Our relationships with others mature. People come and go. Jobs are obtained and lost. The only constant in the midst of the turmoil is our at-one-ment with the Infinite Intelligence.

If we are to understand ourselves and life, we must see beyond everything that is changing. We must attain a state of consciousness that allows us to recognize the Infinite Intelligence as the only intelligence, to understand our oneness with God, the only presence.

Spiritualism points the way to that higher state of consciousness. It enables us to see that man is a soul animated by spirit, a dweller in ever present eternity, co-eternal with God, occupying a physical body on the earthly plane. "Man is not a body with a spirit, but a spirit with a body and a mind to serve him."

Why seek to develop the higher part within one's self? For two reasons. First, so that we may take our place on the higher planes of consciousness in spirit life after passing on. And secondly, that through developing ourselves while still on the earthly plane, we may assist others who may have lost their way. For, in helping others, we help a part of the Infinite Intelligence, a part of ourselves.

Our hearts must go out to all men in every walk of life. We must put ourselves in every man's place so that we may understand his viewpoint and motives. "With true sympathy manifest in our lives, knowledge, as has been said, is born."

Expressing true sympathy produces within us a subtle power, poise. Poise is a great tower of strength to body and to spirit. It cannot be seen in the physical sense, but it controls all of our actions. It enables us to deal with life, not as a temporary stay here on earth, but as an eternal manifestation.

Three attributes; knowledge, sympathy, and poise create success, health, happiness, and true greatness. They allow us to conserve our energy so that each act counts, and each deed accomplishes its purpose. As we develop these qualities through correct and constructive thinking, we will radiate love, health, and success to others.

We will lift ourselves and others.

Additional Reading:

Burroughs, H. Gordon (1962) *Becoming a Spiritualist*, Port City Press.

Spirits Do Not Get Stuck

Today I want to talk about something that bothers me very deeply.

I spoke at an event the other day. Afterward, a woman came up to me in obvious distress. She told me that her father had died a couple of weeks previously. She was afraid that because she hadn't received a sign from him, that he was "stuck" somewhere.

"No," I told her. "Your father is not 'stuck'."

This wasn't the first time someone's come to me with this fear. I don't know how the notion started. Maybe it began with a movie or TV show. I know it's been perpetuated by ghost hunters who think they have to free ghosts by telling them to go to the light.

Let me be perfectly clear. Spirits do not stay on the physical plane after death. I had a Near Death Experience at the age of five and have been in touch with the Spirit World since then. Believe me when I say, SPIRITS DO NOT GET STUCK. When someone dies they go directly to the light. They do not get trapped in their house or on the Earth. They do not wander aimlessly.

Perpetuating this myth brings great stress and worry to the person who loses someone dear. I must then reassure them that their loved one, who has taken their last breath, is on the other side with no pain or discomfort. The person is with others who love them. I know this from experience. No one showed me the way to the light. It was right there in front of my eyes. I had no problem with the crossing over process.

When people asked me about passing, I tell them that our loved ones who have crossed over are sometimes busy with their new adventure or journey. This is a time of transition and exploration. We must be patient. Our love ones will, in time, contact us in some way: a smell, a song, a touch, a symbol, or a dream. And it will happen when you least expect it.

"Our present state is a rudimentary one," W.H. Evans said. "It is for us, though not for the Supreme Mind, a beginning. This world is, as Stewart White's wife, Betty, reminds us in *The Unobstructed Universe*, the 'borning place of the souls,' the place in which the Supreme Mind becomes focused in self-conscious beings endowed with great and wondrous powers. If we catch a glimpse of this and at the time release our oneness with the Supreme Mind, we shall know ourselves as immortal beings."

When dealing with the passing from this world to the next, remember, this life is only the beginning. Loved ones who have passed over to the other side are experiencing the next step in their spiritual journey. Nothing is holding them back.

Additional Reading:

Evans, W.H. (1917) *Constructive Spiritualism*. Two Worlds Publishing Co. Manchester, England

White, Stewart Edward (1940) *The Unobstructed Universe*. Reprinted 1988, Ariel Press

Spiritualism in Today's World

In today's fast paced world, people are so caught up with living day to day, they barely have time to think. Electronic media bombards us with information constantly, but what does it say to us? Buy this. Choose that. Get involved with this drama. Don't ignore this. Never rest. Never be quiet.

What happens when we pause to think? Do we have a philosophy of life? Do our lives have purpose? Do we have goals and direction?

Spiritualism can add focus and direction in today's hectic world by allowing us to see the bigger picture, to see not only our short physical life on Earth, but that we are part of a longer spiritual journey.

All religions have taught about the existence of the soul after death. In early religious history, leaders demonstrated man's contact with the dimension beyond and the continuity of the spirit, but that was lost over time. Religions became more materialistic, focusing more on the physical. Connecting with the spiritual realm by lay people was discouraged, and even forbidden.

In wasn't until Spiritualism began in the 1840s that people were again encouraged to connect with spirits beyond in an effort to demonstrate the existence of the spiritual world. Spiritualists taught that individuality continues, the personality endures after the change we know as death.

Spiritualism is almost 200 years old, and it exists in today's world with a clearly defined philosophy. We find it in the first lines of the poem: "Born I am. I am what I am, A soul immortal, garbed as man," by Alexander Jenkins.

Spiritualism teaches a broad philosophy. It takes all into its arms, and folds into its heart the philosophies of all mankind. If finds the good in all. We are all brothers and sisters.

Spiritualism accepts the presence of a Divine Energy or God. The immortal soul cannot be separated from God, and always manifests with the Divine Energy. God does not condemn us or cast us out of the divine plan. Garbed for the moment as part of mankind, you retain all your experiences along your immortal path. No one can take that away from you.

Spiritualists believe we must all be responsible of our own lives. "As a man thinketh, so is he." Life owes us nothing; we owe the world everything. We get out of the world just what we put into it, nothing more or nothing less. As we sincerely think, so will our actions become. It makes no difference how straight or narrow the way. We are the masters of our fate; the masters of our souls; we are the ones who pave the way. We all make our own heaven or hell. We cannot find happiness until we create happiness; there is no possible way of finding joy unless we create joy.

The full realization of these simple truths makes life a magnificent activity. H. Gordon Burroughs said, "What a marvelous time we are living in at the present moment: the time of challenge, the clear, definite clarion call to humanity to reach up and throw off the shackles of ignorance, selfishness, and woe, and to come into the realization of at-one-ment with God- the realization that all souls are of equal importance to the great, the eternal manifestation of life; that they cannot be lost; that they play their part, well or ill, but have the power within to be masters of the part they are playing."

As Spiritualists, we must teach the non-existence of death. Death, like birth, is just an event in the great eternal plan. All the things through which we pass are experiences along the pathway of soul. We must teach the world peace at all times. It is our place to remain poised and calm in times of stress; to continue to manifest God in action; to meet birth and death as incidents in the great plan of life.

Our goal must be to always serve humanity. We must continue to work with God to attain self-illumination so that we may show the way to others that they may find the truth. In truth, we will walk unafraid, living with God, an "immortal, garbed as man".

Burroughs quoted the old teachers as saying, "Let there be many windows to your soul. One pane cannot catch the thousands of scintillating truths that radiate from the kingdom of God. Lift the blinds of superstition; let the soul open wide the windows through which the truth may enter. Attune your ear to the wordless music of the spheres; and your heart, like a flower seeking the sun, will reach out for truth and a million unseen hands will reach down to help you up to piece-crowned heights. The glory of the firmament Will sustain you."

Additional reading:

Burroughs, H. Gordon (1962) *Becoming a Spiritualist*, Port City Press

Jenkins, Alexander F. (1978) *Am I? in* The National Spiritualist, Feb. 1978 edition, Cassadaga, Florida

Have We Lived Here Before?

Researchers at the University of Virginia began studying reports of past-life memories forty-five years ago. They found that cases in children occur worldwide, although they are more prevalent in cultures that believe in reincarnation. Over 2,500 cases have been investigated.

Ian Stevenson, chairman of the Department of Psychiatry reviewed published case studies in 1960, before starting his own research. He traveled to both India and Ceylon. There, he used a careful, methodical approach to document the phenomena. One of his books was reviewed by the Journal of the American Medical Association in 1975. The reviewer said the past-life evidence was "difficult to explain on any other grounds."

Past-life cases share many common characteristics. Children begin to describe the previous life when they are between 2-3 years old and stop by age 6. Their stories about past lives occur spontaneously, without the aid of hypnosis. Previous lives tend to be as real as the child's present life, although they indicate that there is a time interval between lives. And surprisingly, in 70% of the cases, they died by unnatural means in the past life.

If the child gives enough information, there is an attempt to identify the person of the past life. When cases are investigated, history is obtained from as many people as possible. The previous family is also interviewed to determine how accurate the child is.

Birthmarks and birth defects appear to match wounds that were fatal to the previous person. Stevenson published 200 cases. One example includes a girl with deformed fingers remembering the life of a man whose fingers were cut off. In another example, a boy was born with two birthmarks on his head. A small one in the back and a larger irregular one on his forehead. The person he claimed to have been was murdered by being shot in the head, with wound locations in the areas of the birth marks.

Most children focus on the end of the previous life. 75% give details of the death, especially when it's violent. 20% report memories between lives. Some describe the funeral or staying in the area where they died. One child said, as a man, he stayed for 7 years near the tree where his body was dumped before following his future father home. Others spoke of entering other realms and seeing other entities there.

The children also displayed behaviors associated with the past life. Many had phobia dealing with the means of death. Some acted out scenarios that the previous person lived. Those who were the opposite sex in past life act as the other sex.

Dr. Jim Tucker, the director of the Division of Perceptual Studies, has focused his research on United States cases. Those cases include 57% boys, aged 4 or younger. In 90% of the cases, the person had an unnatural death. In 16 cases where the previous person has been identified, 14 were deceased family members. His most recent book, Return to Life, describes some of those accounts.

Statements made by a child who seems to be remembering a previous life may include:

"You're not my mommy/daddy."

"I have another mommy/daddy."

"When I was big, I …(used to have blue eyes/had a car, etc.)."

"That happened before I was in mommy's tummy."

"I have a wife/husband/children."

"I used to…(drive a truck/live in another town, etc.)"

"I died … (in a car accident/after I fell, etc.)"

"Remember when I ...(lived in that other house/was your daddy, etc.)"

Additional Reading:

Tucker, Jim B. (2008). *Children's Reports of Past-Life Memories: A Review*. Explore 2008; 4:244-248 Elsevier Inc.

Halloween and Spiritualism

The celebration of Halloween began as the ancient festival of Samhain practiced 2,000 years ago by the Celts in the area that is now Great Britain and northern France. The festival marked the harvest and beginning of winter. The Celts believed that on the eve of the new year, which was November 1st for them, the boundary between the worlds of the living and the dead thinned, ghosts of the dead returned to earth.

The presence of the otherworldly spirits, they believed, made it easier for the Druids to make predictions about the future. Their prophecies were an important source of comfort and direction during the cold, dark winter. The Druids built huge bonfires. People came dressed in costumes made of skins and animal heads to offer sacrifices to Celtic gods. When the celebration was over, they re-lit their hearth fires from the sacred fire to help protect them during the long winter.

As the Roman Empire conquered Celtic territory, two Roman festivals were combined with Samhain. Feralia was a day in late October when the Romans commemorated the passing of the dead. The second festival honored Pomona, the Roman goddess of fruit and trees.

Once the Catholic church subjugated the Roman Empire, the pagan celebrations were replaced by All Martyrs Day. In 609 A.D., Pope Boniface IV dedicated the Pantheon in Rome in honor of all Christian martyrs. Pope Gregory III later expanded the festival to include saints as well. The date was moved from May 13 to November 1.

By the 800s, Christianity had spread across Europe. The church made November 2nd All Souls' Day, to honor the dead.

All Souls Day was celebrated with big bonfires, parades, and dressing up in costumes as saints, angels and devils. It was called All-hallows or All-hallowmas. The night before was called All-Hallows Eve. That eventually became Halloween.

Those who follow the ancient traditions believe as the Celts, that Halloween is a time when the veil thins between the world of the living and the dead. This contrasts with the beliefs of Spiritualism. Even though Spiritualists believe in the existence of the two worlds, we do not believe that the connection between the worlds is affected by the position of the Earth in its journey around the sun.

Spiritualists believe in the "communion of spirits and the ministry of angels" as well as "the continuous existence of the human soul." We believe that when the physical body dies, the spirit continues in the spiritual world. The spiritual world can interface with the material world, but that does not require a special day, time or place to happen.

As one who had a childhood near-death experience (NDE) and trained as a medium, I believe the connection between worlds is affected by both personal experience and education. I am fortunate that my NDE makes it easier for me to contact the Spirit World. But even with that experience, I had to receive instruction to become a medium.

Halloween is a celebration that harkens back to ancient days when humans first questioned their existence in the world. It can bring us closer together and maybe bring us closer to the Spirit World, but it doesn't take an ancient festival to reach the other side. It is always here with us.

Section II:

THE HISTORY OF SPIRITUALISM

Hydesville, NY: Part I

The story of Spiritualism begins with a small cabin in a rural town in western New York State. While the Weekmans lived in the house during 1846–7, they heard footsteps in the cellar and loud raps on the floors, doors and walls. They attempted to catch the perpetrator but were never successful. Their experiences continued. At one point, their eight-year-old daughter was wakened in the night by feeling something cold touching her face. Mr. Weekman heard his name called when he was alone. Their servant saw the apparition of a man in the bedroom. Needless to say, the Weekmans did not stay in the cabin long.

In December of 1847, John David Fox with his wife and two daughters, Catherine, aged twelve, and Margaretta, aged fifteen, became the next tenants. The family was frequently disturbed at night with the sounds as of furniture being moved or knocking on the doors and walls. Later, they heard gurgling, as if someone was being choked, and a body falling to the floor. Once, the girls were frightened by a large weight lying across their feet and a cold hand passing over their faces. It became impossible for them to sleep.

Mrs. Fox moved the girls into her room. On March 30th, noises seemed to come from everywhere. Trying to figure out what was happening, Mr. Fox stood on one side of the door and his wife on the other, but the rappings seemed to emanate from the door between them. The next morning was cold and snow had fallen. Wind rattled the sashes. Thinking they might be loose, Mr. Fox shook them. It was at that time that Catherine noticed the rappings seemed to respond. Every time Mr. Fox shook a window sash, the raps would imitate the number.

What had been terrifying the night before, now seemed more like a mystery to solve. Catherine snapped her fingers and said, "Here, old splitfoot, do as I do." To everyone's surprise, the spirit responded with as many raps as she had snapped. Margaretta joined in, clapping her hands a number of times. "Now do as I do," she said. "Count one, two, three, four." The rappings correctly responded. Catherine varied the game by making snapping motions without producing any sound. The rappings again responded correctly. Catherine said, "Look, mother, it can see as well as hear!"

Mrs. Fox put the mysterious rappings to a test. "Count ten," she said. The rappings responded correctly. "How many children have I?" she added. "Seven," they replied. At first, she thought it was a mistake because she only had six living children. Then she realized the response included her child who had passed away. The family continued to test the mysterious rappings further. The ages of all her children were tapped out to order.

And that is how the communication began.

Additional Reading:

Boddington, Harry. "The University of Spiritualism." iBooks. https://itun.es/us/M-oH1.l

Hydesville, NY: Part II

The experiences of the Fox family while living in the Hydesville cabin have been written about numerous times. Part I of my blog was based on Harry Boddington's account. But we have affidavits that were published within weeks of the original experiences on March 31, 1848. These personal testimonies were told to an attorney from a nearby town and published by E.E. Lewis in 1848.

In Margaret Fox's statement, she explained how they had moved into the house December 11, 1847. They first heard the strange rapping noises two weeks before the testimony was taken. The entire family slept in the same room and all heard the noises together.

"The first night that we heard the rapping, we all got up and lit a candle; and searched all over the house," she said. "The noise continued while we were hunting and was heard near the same place all the time. It was not very loud, yet it produced a jar of the bedsteads and chairs, that could be felt by placing our hands on the chair or while we were in bed. It was a feeling of a tremulous motion, more than a sudden jar. It seemed as if we could feel it jar while we were standing on the floor. It continued this night until we went to sleep. I did not go to sleep until nearly 12 o'clock. The noise continued to be heard every night."

On Friday, March 31st, they heard the noises earlier in the evening. This was the first time the girls tried to mimic the sounds by snapping their fingers. It was then that they found the rapping would also mimic their movements. "Then I spoke and said to the noise, 'Count ten,' and it made ten strokes or noises," Mrs. Fox said. "Then I asked the ages of my different children successively, and it gave a number of raps, corresponding to the ages of my children."

When she asked if it was human, it did not respond. But when she asked it to respond with two raps if it was spirit, it rapped twice distinctly. "When I asked how many years old it was?" she stated, "it rapped 31 times; that it was a male; that it had left a family of five children; that it had two sons and three daughters, all living. I asked if it left a wife? and it rapped. If its wife was then living? no rapping; if she was dead? and the rapping was distinctly heard how long she had been dead? and it rapped twice."

At that moment, Ms. Fox suggested they call the neighbors to come witness the rapping. Mrs. Redfield, their next-door neighbor came immediately. At first, she thought it was a joke or a trick. "It told her age exactly," Mrs. Fox said. "She would then call her husband, and he came; and the same questions were asked over again, and the answers were the same as before."

Mr. Redfield invited Mr. Duesler and several others to the house. Mrs. Fox said, "A great many questions were asked over, and the same answers given as before. Mr. Duesler then called in Mr. and Mrs. Hyde; they came, and also Mr. and Mrs. Jewell. Mr. Duesler asked many questions and got the answers."

Additional Reading:

Lewis, E.E. (1848) *A report of the Mysterious Noises Heard in the House of Mr. John D. Fox in Hydesville, Arcadia, Wayne County.* Authenticated by the Certificates and Confirmed by Statements of the Citizens of That Place and Vicinity. Power Press of Shepard and Reed, Rochester, NY

Hydesville, NY: Part III

In his testimony, William Duesler confirmed that he lived within "a few rods of the house in which these noises [were] heard." At first, he ridiculed the idea and laughed at his wife for being interested in such a ridiculous idea. "I told her it was all nonsense, and that we would find out the cause of the noise, and that it could easily be accounted for." He accompanied about a dozen people to the house at nine-o-clock in the evening. "Some were so frightened that they did not want to go into the room," he said. "I heard the rapping which they had spoken of, distinctly. I felt the bedstead jar when the sound was produced."

According to Mrs. Fox, Mr. Duelser was the person who continued to question the mysterious entity about its demise. He named all the neighbors and asked if any of them had injured the spirit. Mrs. Fox stated that, "Mr. Duesler asked it some questions, the same as I had, and got the same answers. He asked if it was murdered? and it answered in the usual way; and if the murderer could be brought to justice? and there was no sound: and then, if he could be punished by the law? and there was no rapping. He then asked, 'if this murderer cannot be punished by the law, manifest it by the noise?' and the noise was repeated."

Through Mr. Duesler's questioning, they found that the subject had been murdered five years previously. In the testimony, the murderer was only identified as a Mr. --- ----. Mr Duesler asked if Mr.--- ---- (naming a person who had formerly lived in the house,) had injured it, and it made three unusually loud knocks and jarred the bedstead more than it had done before, affirming the question. More questions determined that the spirit was killed for five hundred dollars.

Elizabeth Jewell, Wife of David Jewell, who lived a short distance from the house said she arrived Friday evening, March 31st about 10 o'clock P.M. "When I got there," she said. "William Duesler was asking questions in relation to the murder. It was asked if different individuals had committed this murder, (naming separately different people who had lived in that house, also some who lived in the neighborhood;) to all of which questions there were no answers, until it was asked if --- ----was the man who murdered it? and it answered immediately by rapping. The rapping was quite loud."

Mr. Duesler continued his questioning, asking about Mr. --- -----'s wife and a Lucretia Pulver who worked for the homeowner at the time. He found that both of the women were gone for the night. He said, "I asked if the body was put in the cellar? and it rapped. I then asked if it was buried in the different parts of the cellar? and to all my questions there was no rapping until I asked if it was near the center? and the rapping was heard.

At that point, many decided it was time to go home. Mrs. Fox said, "I and my family all left the house but my husband. I went to Mrs. Redfield's and staid all night: my children staid at some of the other neighbors. My husband and Mr. Redfield staid in the house all that night."

Elizabeth Jewell said, "I never have been a believer in supernatural appearances on earth, and never have seen or heard anything before which I could not account for in some way or other. This I am wholly at a loss to account for, unless it is a supernatural appearance. I have been acquainted with Mr. Fox and family some time, and cheerfully certify that I never saw anything in their conduct, or heard anything about them, that would lead me to suppose that they would be guilty of carrying on any trickery in order to deceive the public: on the contrary, I have always looked upon them as honest, upright people, and good neighbors."

Additional Reading:

Lewis, E.E. (1848) *A report of the Mysterious Noises Heard in the House of Mr. John D. Fox in Hydesville, Arcadia, Wayne County*. Authenticated by the Certificates and Confirmed by Statements of the Citizens of That Place and Vicinity. Power Press of Shepard and Reed, Rochester, NY

Hydesville, NY: Part IV

After they discovered that a murder could have taken place and a body might be buried in the cellar, William Duesler and Charles Redfield took a candle and examined the cellar. Mr. Duesler said, "I told him to place himself in different parts of the cellar, and as he did so, I asked the question, if a person was over the place where it was buried? and I got no answer, until he got over a certain place in the cellar, when it rapped. He then stepped to one side, and when I asked the question, there was no noise. This we repeated several times, and we found that whenever he stood over this one place, the rapping was heard, and whenever be moved away from that place, there was no rapping in answer to my questions. Mr. Redfield said that he could hear the noise himself."

Walter Scotten confirmed that the noise in the cellar came from the ground. "Some thought it was on one side, and some on the other," he said. "We could hardly tell in what direction it come from. It did not sound like any noise that could be made by rapping or striking, either on the floor or on the ground. I have since tried to make the same noise in many different ways but have never succeeded in imitating it." He was in the house about a half hour with Stephen Smith, his wife, Mrs. Fox, Mrs. Losey, Mr. Wm. D. Storer and two girls. "There had been digging in the cellar at the time I was there. They had dug about two feet and a half, I should think. There was a good deal of water in the hole, which they said had prevented them from digging anymore."

They continued their questioning and found that the murdered man was a peddler. The peddler's wife had died, but he still had children who were living. They were unsuccessful at trying to determine the dead man's name, only identifying two initials: C. and B. According to Mr. Duesler, "There were a good many more questions asked on that night, by myself and others; which I do not now remember. They were all answered readily in the same way. I staid in the house until about 12 o'clock, and then came home. Mr. Redfield and Mr. Fox staid in the house that night."

John Fox insisted that they couldn't find any natural cause for the events in the house. "We have searched in every nook and corner in and about the house, at different times, to ascertain if possible whether anything or any body was secreted there, that could make the noise, and have never been able to find anything which explained the mystery."

John was anxious and concerned because the rapping attracted hundreds of people, and none of the family were able to get any work done. He hoped a cause would soon be found and their lives could return to normal. He said, "The digging in the cellar will be resumed as soon as the water settles; and then it can be ascertained whether there are any indications of a body ever having been buried there; and if there are, I shall have no doubt but what this is a supernatural appearance."

Mrs. Fox said, "I am not a believer in haunted houses or supernatural appearances. I am very sorry that there has been so much excitement about it. It has been a great deal of trouble to us. It was our misfortune to live here at this time; but I am willing and anxious that the truth should he known, and that a true statement should be made. I cannot account for these noises; all that I know is, that they have been heard repeatedly, as I have stated. "

Even though many excavations were made in the cellar, no skeleton was ever found buried in the floor. It wasn't until 50 years later that an article in the Boston Journal, November 22, 1904, stated, "The skeleton of the man supposed to have caused the rappings first heard by the Fox sisters in 1848 has been found in the walls of the house..." The bones were discovered by school students who were investigating part of the old cellar wall that had crumbled. In an editorial that appeared in the Journal of the American Society for Psychical research, a physician had examined the bones and reported "he found a number of bones there, but that there were only a few ribs with odds and ends of bones and among them a superabundance of some and a deficiency of others. Among them also were some chicken bones." Despite some people's claims, the peddler's remains were never found in the house.

After the initial events in Hydesville, Margaret and Catherine were sent to Rochester. Catherine went to the house of her sister Leah Fish, and Margaret to the home of their brother David. The rappings followed them, but that is another story.

Additional reading:

Cadwallader, M.E. (1922) *Hydesville in History.* Chicago: Progressive Thinker.

Editorial (1909) Journal of the American Society for Psychical Research. March, 191 issue.

Lewis, E.E. (1848) A Report of the Mysterious Noises Heard in the House of Mr. John D. Fox in Hydesville, Arcadia, Wayne County. Authenticated by the Certificates and Confirmed by Statements of the Citizens of That Place and Vicinity. Power Press of Shepard and Reed, Rochester, NY

National Spiritualist Association of Churches

Modern Spiritualism evolved in response to a series of events that began in the mid-eighteenth century. Emanuel Swedenborg, who wrote of his visions between 1744 and 1772, described the Spirit World in detail. Less than a century later, Edward Irving's spiritual manifestations during the 1830s and the Shakers practices from 1837 to 1844 paved the way for an interest in the rapping communication between the Fox family and a spirit in Hydesville, NY in 1848. This led to the belief that our interaction with the Spirit World is part of Natural Law and not miraculous or supernatural, which distinguishes Modern from Ancient Spiritualism.

The National Spiritualist Association of Churches (NSAC) first formed as the National Spiritualist Association of the United States of America (NSA) in Chicago in 1893 to promote Spiritualism and educate the public. One goal was to help non-Spiritualists distinguish genuine from fraudulent mediumship, which was rapidly proliferating at the time. They also functioned as a foundation to increase communication among Spiritualists and prevent legal prosecution of spirit mediums under fortune telling and medical licensing laws.

NSA's first leaders were W. H. Bach, Harrison D. Barrett, Luther V. Moulton, James Martin Peebles, and Cora L. V. Scott. In 1899, a six-article "Declaration of Principles" was adopted by many Spiritualist groups. Three other articles were added at later dates.

1. We believe in Infinite Intelligence
2. We believe that the phenomena of Nature, both physical and spiritual, are the expression of Infinite Intelligence
3. We affirm that a correct understanding of such expression and living in accordance therewith constitute true religion
4. We affirm that the existence and personal identity of the individual continue after the change called death
5. We affirm that communication with the so-called dead is a fact, scientifically proven by the phenomena of Spiritualism
6. We believe that the highest morality is contained in the Golden Rule: "Do unto others as you would have them do unto you."
7. We affirm the moral responsibility of the individual, and that we make our own happiness or unhappiness as we obey or disobey Nature's physical and spiritual laws. 1899
8. We affirm that the doorway to reformation is never closed against any soul here or hereafter. 1909
9. We affirm that the precept of Prophesy and Healing are Divine attributes proven through Mediumship. 1944

The NSAC has two educational institutes, the Morris Pratt Institute in Milwaukee and The Center for Spiritualist Studies in Lily Dale, New York.

Morris Pratt Institute was built and designed by the founder as a temple and a school for Spiritualism in 1888. At the Ninth Annual convention of the NSAC in Washington, D.C., Morris and Zulema Pratt presented a letter to the NSAC offering them the property to be utilized "for educational purposes."

The Center for Spiritualist Studies in Lily Dale is located on the grounds of the NSAC-chartered Lily Dale Assembly, the world's largest Spiritualist camp. The goal of the center is the training of Spiritualist Clergy Teachers, Mediums and Healers.

Additional Reading:

Website of the NCAC http://nsac.org

Spiritualists' National Union

Spiritualism spread from the United States to England in the early 1850s and the first Spiritualist church was established in Yorkshire in 1853. The Yorkshire Spiritualist Telegraph became their first newspaper, published in 1855. By the early 1880s many spiritualist organizations and churches had sprung up around Britain. Leading medium, Emma Hardinge Britten, founded a weekly spiritualist journal called *Two Worlds* in 1887.

By the 1890s, Spiritualism had so many supporters it became clear that some sort of organization was needed to help unite the churches and societies. Britten took the lead and spread the idea of a creating a federation. The Spiritualists' National Federation was founded in 1890 and was succeeded by the Spiritualists' National Union (SNU) which incorporated in 1901.

Over its history, the SNU organized test cases regarding the legal status of spiritualists. Since mediumship was considered to violate such laws as the Vagrancy Act of 1824 and the Witchcraft Act of 1735, the SNU Union campaigned against these laws for many years, eventually repealing them with the Fraudulent mediums Act in 1951. The act legalized the practice of mediumship unless it was shown that a medium was profiting financially from a fraudulent service.

The SNU also conducted more everyday services, such as organizing war memorial services in the wake of WWI. It organized educational courses on spiritualism-related subjects and participated in scientific research into mediumship. It acquired the publication *Psychic News*, which it ran until 2011.

Today, the SNU supports about 340 Spiritualist churches and centers throughout Great Britain. Approximately 11,500 people pay an annual subscription for membership through their organizations. The SNU also owns The Arthur Findley College and Barbanell Conference Center. The college houses thousands of original documents and historical artifacts associated with Spiritualism and psychic science. It supports the training of spiritual healers, spirit mediums, public speakers and teachers.

In 2009, the Spiritualists' National Union International (SNUI) was set up as a branch of the SNU. It provides online access to information, education, and training to enable members around the globe. Tutors offer opportunities to take part in online services and new students are welcomed into an international community.

Additional Reading:

Website of the SNU: https://www.snu.org.uk/

International Spiritualist Federation

World Spiritualist meetings were first held in the late 1880s, including one in Barcelona (1888), and in Paris (1889). At that time, unsuccessful attempts were made to form an international federation. The onset of WWI and the many deaths that followed led to the rapid development of Spiritualism around the world. That provided new impetus to create a unified organization. After the war, additional meetings were held in Paris, London, The Hague, Barcelona and Glasgow. The International Spiritualists Federation (ISF) was officially established in 1923.

Unfortunately, World War II stopped all international work. The records of the original organization stored in Paris were destroyed. It wasn't until 1947 that a special conference was held in Bournemouth, England with a small number of delegates from Great Britain, France, South Africa, Canada and Sweden. Congresses have been hosted by many countries since 1948 including, Sweden, France, Denmark, Scotland, England, Holland, Spain, and the United States.

The aim of the ISF is "to reveal that Spiritual Nature of Mankind which harmonizes with Natural Law," and to "promote the advancement, by educational means, and the diffusion throughout the world, of a knowledge of the science and philosophy of Spiritualism/Spiritism." They see Spiritualism as a world movement to educate all about the reality of spirit and the survival of the human personality after physical death. Mediums are used to demonstrate not only continuity of spirit but also the purpose of our existence.

As part of its commitment, the ISF has set up a Scientific Forum and provides teams of teachers to visit different countries, and train mediums, healers and speakers to use their gifts. They consider the greatest field of exploration remaining to science to be that of the mind. Most scientists see the mind as purely physical, but mediumship has demonstrated that there is a non-physical component that survives the death of the physical body.

The Federation has published the journal, *Yours Fraternally*, since 1948 under various guises. It includes news from members around the world. Over the years some of the greatest names in Spiritualism have appeared within its pages.

Today, membership is open to groups as well as individuals. Groups may include societies, associations, churches, and educational assemblies. The only requirement is that they accept all the Principles and rules of the ISF. The Committee must be satisfied that the group´s aims, objectives and activities do not conflict with the purposes of the ISF and are consistent with membership requirements.

Additional Reading:

ISF Website: https://www.theisf.com/

Arthur Findlay College

Arthur Findlay was born into a staunch Christian family in Glasgow in 1883. He was first employed as an accountant in the shipping business and later as a stockbroker. He served as a local justice of the peace, and during WWI dedicated his time to the Red Cross. In 1913, he received the *Most Excellent Order of the British Empire* for his war work.

Findlay became a student of comparative religion at the age of seventeen, even though his parents burned his collection of books to discourage his interest. His first experience with Spiritualism occurred in 1918 when he passed by a Spiritualist church, became curious, and went inside. Findlay was skeptical about the mediumship he'd witnesses, but when invited by Duncan McPherson to attend a séance with John Sloan the following day, he decided to go. A message from his father during the séance convinced him to investigate Spiritualism in greater depth.

In 1920, Findlay founded the Glasgow Society for Psychical Research. He became Founder and Chairman of the International Institute for Psychical Research, Co-founder of the *Psychic News*, and Honorary member of the American Foundation for Psychical Research, Edinburgh Psychic College, and the Institute of Psychic Writers and Artists. At one time he was President of the Spiritualists' National Union.

"Psychic science, however, is opening to us a new universe, a universe of etheric substance, governed by mind, and only when orthodox science condescends to examine this new universe revealed to us through mediumship, can it possibly hope to get a true perspective of the universe as a whole," Findlay said in a letter to *The Times* in 1932.

When he retired in 1923, he purchased Stansted Hall in Stansted, England, a manor house built in 1871. The idea of creating a Spiritualist College there and donating it to the Spiritualist's National Union (SNU) arose in 1945. A will was drawn up and in 1954 the SNU accepted the proposed bequest of Stansted Hall with an endowment. This was followed by a later gift in the form of stock to be used for furnishing and decorating the building. In 1964, a year after the death of his wife, Findlay transferred the Hall, grounds and endowment to the SNU. He passed on to the Spirit World in July 1964.

Today, Arthur Findlay College is a residential center where students can study Spiritualist philosophy and religious practice, Spiritualist healing and awareness, spiritual and psychic unfolding and other related disciplines. Courses, lectures and demonstrations are all offered by leading teachers. The college also features a library, museum, lake, beautiful grounds, recreational facilities and full-board accommodations.

Additional Reading:

College Website: https://www.arthurfindlaycollege.org/

Colored Spiritualist Association of Churches

African Americans were attracted to the Spiritualist movement in the years following the formation of the National Spiritualist Association of Churches (NSAC) in 1893. A few talented mediums emerged. Unfortunately, in the 1920s Jim Crow laws and calls for segregation put pressure on the NSAC. In response, African American members were organized into "colored" auxiliary societies of the NSAC.

When racial tensions increased following World War I, the NSAC leadership worked to create a separate all-black Spiritualist organization. The appointed president, Joseph P. Whitwell, led the first meeting held in Cleveland, Ohio on April 21, 1925. Twenty delegates attended the meeting, but six withdrew to protest the establishment of a segregated organization. The remaining delegates formed the National Colored Spiritualist Association of Churches (NCSAC). At a second national meeting in 1926, they adopted a new constitution, following the NSAC's "Declaration of Principles."

"Religion is alive and well," Joseph P. Whitwell said. "A correct understanding of the laws of nature on the physical, mental and spiritual planes of life and living in accordance therewith will unfold the highest aspirations and attributes of the Soul, which is the correct function of True Religion."

The NCSAC included churches in Chicago, Detroit, Philadelphia, New York City, and elsewhere. By 1938 there were fifty-one Black Spiritualist churches in Chicago alone.

Most Black Spiritualist churches combined Spiritualism, including using Spirit Guides, with Protestant and Catholic beliefs. Church names identified the Christian orientation of congregations. For example, the Divine Israel Spiritual Church identified with Black Baptist churches and the Infant Jesus of Prague Spiritual Church featured Catholic saints on their altars.

The NCSAC eventually divided into two camps. One group included the historical African American Spiritualist churches, such as the African Cultural Nationalist Universal Hagar's Spiritual Church, Pentecostal Spiritual Assemblies of Christ, and Metropolitan Spiritual Churches of Christ. The second group included the Spiritual Churches of New Orleans. They were a diverse group of denominations descended from the followers of medium Leafy Anderson. Their beliefs were based on Black feminism and the Gospel of John, where Jesus encounters the Samaritan woman.

The Civil Rights movement of the 1960s eliminated the need to segregate churches. The NCSAC continued into the 1970s but its status today is unknown.

Additional Reading:

Holms, A. Campbell. (1927) *The Fundamental Facts of Spiritualism*. The Occult Press.

Melton, J. Gordon. (1999) *Encyclopedia of American Religions*. 6th edition. Detroit, Gale Research

Guillory, MS (2016) Conscious Concealment: The Repression and Expression of African American Spiritualism. In *Histories of a Hidden God: Concealment and revelation in Western Gnostic, Escoteric and Mystical Traditions*. Ed. April D. DeConick & Grant Adamson. Routledge.

Lily Dale: Home to Spiritualism

Hidden away in northwestern New York state is a quiet hamlet named Lily Dale. The idyllic community, composed of Victorian homes and uniquely decorated cottages, overlooks the east side of Cassadaga Lake. At first glance, it would appear to be a vacationer's paradise, but the entrance sign, "City of Light," reveals its true origins. Lily Dale is the largest community of Spiritualists in the country.

The seeds of Lily Dale were planted in 1844, when William Johnson invited a mesmerist named Dr. Moran from Vermont to come to Laona, NY to lecture. After the visit, Johnson and his group began to experiment with Dr. Moran's techniques. Group member, Jeremiah Carter, became entranced. Through him, a Dr. Hedges spoke to those present. He gave messages from the Spirit World and practiced laying on of hands. After spiritual communication was established in Hydesville, NY by the Fox sisters, the Laona group was encouraged to continue. They formed the First Spiritualist Society of Laona in 1855.

In 1873, Jeremiah Carter was encouraged by spirits to hold a camp meeting at the nearby farm of Willard Alden (located just outside the gates of Lily Dale). The group met there for summer picnics and camp meetings until Alden's passing in 1879. It was then that the group purchased 20 acres of land.

Men and women worked to clear the area and make forest trails. They had financial problems but were not deterred. A Lyceum formed in 1881, and a permanent auditorium that would seat 1200 was built in 1883. The camp went through several name changes until 1906 when it was named The Lily Dale Assembly because of the abundance of lilies on the lake.

Marion Skidmore, daughter of William Johnson, was one of the main founders of Lily Dale. She was an ardent advocate for women's suffrage, a liberal thinker, and friend of Susan B. Anthony. Her collection of books formed the foundation for the Marion Skidmore Library in Lily Dale, the world's largest collection of Spiritualist and psychic books.

Today, Lily Dale is a community of over 160 private residences, two hotels, guest houses, bookstores, two eateries and a café. Between the last weekend in June and Labor Day, for a small admission fee, visitors can attend many events. They include medium demonstrations, religious services, workshops, thought exchange meetings and healing services. There are also areas for camping, picnicking, swimming and hiking.

Additional seminars are offered on mediumships, spiritualist studies and related topics. Well-known guests have included Deepak Chopra, Dr. Wayne Dyer, and John Edward.

Additional Reading:

Lily Dale's History: www.ronnagy.net

Lily Dale: A Place of Magic

Lily Dale is a hamlet located on the east side of Cassadaga Lake in southwestern New York state. Incorporated in 1879 as the Cassadaga Lake Free Association, it was first a camp and meeting place for Spiritualists and other free thinkers. It eventually became the Lily Dale Assembly in 1906, with the purpose of furthering science, philosophy and Spiritualism.

I first visited Lily Dale in August of 2004. At that time, I was new to the concept of Spiritualism and mediumship. I had mustered the courage to go to Fredonia, NY to take my first mediumship classes with Rev. Leonard Young. After class one day, he announced that we were having dinner at the house of a friend in Lily Dale. My first thoughts were, what and where is this place? I have to admit that I was a little skeptical about visiting a town full of Spiritualists. But as I entered the grounds and strolled around the lake, I was overwhelmed by calming energy.

I had a connection with the Spirit World since having a near death experience at the age of five. I soon discovered Lily Dale was a place where this kind of activity was wide open and accepted. I was really intrigued by Harmony House located in the center of town. It was built in 1895 and was originally the Temple of Health and the site of healing services in the early 1900s. The current owners have renamed it in honor of Andrew Jackson Davis and his Harmonial Philosophy, but it still retains its aura of healing and peace.

That didn't prepare me for my visit to the current Healing Temple which was opened in 1955. The new temple was dedicated to be a place of peace to all those who come to renew their energy through healing, meditation and prayer. I was truly amazed when I first entered the building. I had never had an experience with spiritual healing, and I was changed by my experience there.

Lily Dale was where I first learned about Spiritualism and what it truly meant. I remember going into the Maplewood hotel and seeing all the precipitated paintings. These are works of art which appear on canvas without the use of human hands during a séance. All the pieces are very professional looking and some very large. I could not believe that they were done by the Spirit World.

I next visited Inspiration Stump. Found at the end of a quiet trail in the Leolyn Woods, the old stump has been the site of mediumship demonstrations and services since 1898. My first time walking down the path was one of wonder. I thought of all the people who had demonstrated there and were true to their beliefs in Spiritualism. Today, I find that sitting alone in silence at the Inspiration Stump always restores my energy.

I watched numerous mediums demonstrate at Lily Dale, and I must admit, I was in awe. For the first time, I felt I had found a place with likeminded people. Later, I read that Susan B. Anthony was supposed to have given a speech at Lake Chautauqua, but when they turned her down, Lily Dale opened its doors to her. It has also been said that Sir Arthur Conan Doyle and Harry Houdini used to sit on the porch of one of the guest houses, involved in conversations about life beyond death.

Lily Dale is certainly a place that makes you look within yourself and trust your inner feelings and thoughts. It is a place that is one with the Spirit World. When I think of all the great Spiritualists who walked the very grounds that exist today, I realize what they had to give up to follow their faith. The library offers a large collection of books on Spiritualism. Reading about subjects like inspirational writing, automatic writing, mediumship, spirit guides, home circles, physical mediumship, and mental mediumship, opened my mind to what is possible.

If you have never been to Lily Dale, I urge you to make a trip there just once in your life. Lily Dale's year-round population is about 275. During Summer, they offer classes, workshops, public church services and **mediumship** demonstrations, lectures, and private appointments with mediums. Take advantage of what they have to offer. **I'm sure some part of you will be changed in a special way, just as I was changed.**

International Women's Day: Women Spiritualists

I'd like to celebrate International Women's Day by honoring some of the women who were involved not only with women's rights but with the early Spiritualist movement. You may remember my blogs about Hydesville, NY and the Fox family. In 1848 the Fox sisters became part of a new spiritual revolution when they began communicating with the Spirit World using rapping sounds. They soon moved to Rochester, NY, where they became acquainted with Amy and Isaac Post, a Quaker couple.

Through the Posts, the Fox sisters met and formed a spiritual group of five women (three of them Quakers): Lucretia Mott, her sister Martha Coffin Wright, Elizabeth Caddy Stanton, Mary Ann McClintock and Jane Hunt. They met in McClintock's parlor where the spirits gave them support and approval through rapping messages. It is not surprising that they became important figures in establishing women's rights.

Lucretia Mott was born in Massachusetts and attended boarding school in New York where she stayed on to work as a teaching assistant until she married her husband, James. She was an active abolitionist but was one of many women excluded from the World Anti-Slavery Convention in 1840 because of her gender. By 1848, she was actively working for women's equality by helping write the Declaration of Sentiments for the first women's rights meeting, the Seneca Falls Convention. As a Quaker preacher, her speaking abilities allowed her to become a respected abolitionist, feminist, and reformer. She helped promote equality in marriage, such as women's property rights and rights to their earnings. She worked with Elizabeth Cady

Stanton to make divorce easier to obtain and to safeguard women's custody of their children.

Elizabeth Cady Stanton was one of eleven children born to attorney and judge Daniel Cady in Johnstown, NY. She was a suffragist and civil rights activist. She helped organize the Seneca Falls Convention and formed the National Women's Loyal League with Susan B. Anthony in 1863. She advocated liberal divorce laws and freedom of reproduction. Although she became marginalized later in life, she helped bring about the passage of the 19th Amendment which gave all citizens the right to vote.

Mary Ann McClintock and her husband Thomas were founding members of the Western New York Anti-Slavery Society. Mary Ann helped organize the Seneca Falls Convention and draft the Declaration of Sentiments. She and Thomas were very active in the local Hicksite Quaker community and led the Progressive Friends or Friends of Human Progress.

At 33 years of age, Jane Hunt married and became stepmother to three of her husband's older children. With encouragement from her husband, she became involved with the women's rights movement when several Quaker women invited Lucretia Mott to speak to their group. Jane offered her house for the protest meeting. It was around Hunts' tea table that they drafted a notice about, "A Convention to discuss the social, civic and religious condition and rights of Woman will be held in the Wesleyan Chapel at Seneca Falls, N. Y., on Wednesday and Thursday, the 19th and 20th of July. . . ." Without that gathering there would have been no Seneca Falls Convention.

Additional Reading:

Braude, Ann (2001) Radical Spirits: Spiritualism and Women's Rights in Nineteenth Century America. Indiana University Press, Bloomington, IN

The Rap, Winter 2017 edition, Open Door Sanctuary, Victoria, BC. www.firstspiritualists.com

Precipitated Spirit Paintings: Part I

Precipitated Spirit Paintings or Portraits were produced by spiritualist mediums in the early 20th century. Unlike other forms of spiritual communication, such as spirit writing where spirits guide the medium's hand, during spirit painting the medium doesn't touch the canvas while the painting materializes.

Spirit Portraits were produced during an event similar to a séance. A blank canvas or paper was stretched over a wooden frame. Oil paints were usually present, but not paintbrushes. Usually, the medium and the person requesting the portrait were present in the room, but other observers could take part. Some, or all, of the participants were asked to touch the canvas with their hands or fingers.

The one wishing to contact the deceased person would concentrate on the task and was not required to tell the medium who they wished to contact. The Spirit Portrait gradually appeared on the canvas or paper, taking anywhere between fifteen minutes to an hour to fully take form.

The oldest recorded Spirit Portrait occurred in the mid-16th century, decades before the beginning of Spiritualism. The image of Mexico's Lady of Guadalupe miraculously appeared on the cloak of a man named Juan Diego. The Vatican conducted research on the image and concluded that no signs of human creation appeared to exist. The blue pigment used to create the image could not be identified or reproduced. The agave-fiber cloak which should have decayed in a few years still exists and is on display today at the Basilica of Guadalupe in Mexico City.

Some Precipitated Spirit Paintings of the 20th century can be found on display in the Maplewood Hotel in Lily Dale, New York.

Located sixty miles south of Buffalo, Lily Dale is the oldest and largest community of Spiritualists in the world. Their collection includes portraits by the Campbell Brothers and Bangs Sisters.

CAMPBELL BROTHERS

The Campbell Brothers were not brothers. Many believe they were a gay couple who had to hide their sexual orientation at a time when it would have been condemned. Allan B. Campbell and Charles Campbell (born Charles Shourds) lived at Lily Dale but travelled widely. Their mediumship included slate writing and spirit typewriting as well as Spirit Portraits produced in pastel and oil.

One of the Campbell Brothers most impressive Spirit Portraits is of Azur, Allan's spirit guide. In 1898, they conducted a session in a room that contained enough light for those present to witness the phenomena. To ensure there was no trickery, invited guests were encouraged to place personal markings on the back of the 40" x 60" canvas. During the process, Allan became entranced and Azur spoke through him. The guests witnessed the gradual development of the painting on the canvas. It was completed in 90 minutes. Witnesses also noticed that the star behind Azur's appeared right before their eyes.

Allen died and 1919 and Charles in 1926, leaving behind several notable spirit paintings.

Additional Reading:

Ron Nagy's website:

http://ronnagy.net/ronsblog/2010/09/identifying-a-precipitated-spirit-painting/

Buckland, Raymond (2005) The Spirit Book: The Encyclopedia of Clairvoyance, Channeling and Spiritual Communication. Visible Ink Press, Canton, MI

Precipitated Spirit Paintings: Part II

THE BANGS SISTERS

The Bangs Sisters, Elizabeth (Lizzie) and May, were born in the early 1860s. Their father was a tinsmith and mother, Meroe, a medium. By the 1870s, the sisters were conducting séances in the Chicago area. Messages from the dead appeared on slates, musical instruments were played by spirits and furniture moved.

Despite being arrested for "doing business without a license" in 1881, the sisters became prominent Chicago mediums by 1888. That led to a dramatic arrest in April of that year when two plainclothes detectives attended one of their séances. They claimed to have found a satchel filled with muslin shrouds, whiskers, wigs, and a variety of make-up. They became the "notorious" Bangs Sisters. In the 1890s, a Chicago grand jury tried to indict them, but failed on technicalities. That led to the passage of an Illinois bill that prohibited anyone "from impersonating the spirits of the dead, commonly known as spirit-medium séances, on penalty of fine and imprisonment."

The Bangs Sisters continued with their careers using slate writing. Blank paper was placed between two slates and the slates were bound together with twine or rubber bands. An ink bottle was located nearby. Messages would appear on the paper while it was bound between the slates.

The first precipitated painting was demonstrated by the sisters in 1894. Spirit Portraits became extremely controversial. Some declared them to be hoaxes, but in most cases the sisters had no prior photograph of the spirit subject to work from. Although oil paints were usually present during the séance, the portraits resemble pastels or modern airbrush paintings. They often have a powdery appearance and sometimes appear to be embedded in the canvas. The portraits also changed over time, for example, eyes first appeared closed and spontaneously opened later.

The Bangs Sisters had residences in Lily Dale, NY and Camp Chesterfield, IN as well as their Chicago home. In a 1908 Chesterfield demonstration, a blank canvas was set on the stage before a large audience. Waves of mist traveled over the canvas. "Soon the outline bust form of a person began to appear in the center of the canvas, features becoming more distinct along with the hair and face and, slowly, the entire form of a young girl was clearly distinguishable for all to see."

The eyes changed from closed to open, and when it was complete, a man in the audience, Mr. Alford, recognized the portrait as that of his deceased daughter, Audrey. When the painting of Audrey was originally precipitated, there was a locket around her neck and she held flowers. When the portrait was donated to Camp Chesterfield, both had dematerialized.

The Bangs Sisters created hundreds of portraits during their demonstrations. Some are on display at both Lily Dale and Camp Chesterfield today.

Additional Reading:

Heagerty, N Riley (2016) Portraits from Beyond: The Mediumship of the Bang Sisters. White Crow Productions, Ltd.

Spirit Photography: Part I

Humans have always questioned their place in the universe. Ancient monuments like Stonehenge reflect our attempt to understand the cycles of the sun and stars. Even more ancient cave paintings reflect our primitive effort to understand our world. It is not surprising that we would try to penetrate the "veil of death" and obtain evidence that the departed are not dead but have only changed their state of being. Necromancy, magic, and sorcery were all used in an attempt to pierce the shroud of mystery which envelopes death.

Spiritualism developed in Victorian times to demonstrate that life continues after death. Mediums called to the spirits to make their presence known through rappings, levitations of objects, visions, trances, possessions, direct voices, spirit writings, and automatic writings. Although these methods could have been used over the centuries, spirit photography wasn't possible until chemicals became commercially availability for silver photographic processes, including daguerreotype. With this technique, photographers could capture spirit images on film.

At first, plates were used to create images. Because plates were expensive, images were sometimes cleaned off and the plate used for further exposures. If the cleaning was not thorough enough, a faint image of the previous picture was occasionally left. Of course, critics used that fact to question the credibility of early spirit-photos. But in 1874, Kennett created gelatino-bromide dry plates. They were so cheap that no one bothered to re-coat and reuse them.

Spiritualists who pursued spirit-photography were mostly located in the United States, Great Britain, and France, with the earliest experiments taking place in the 1860s. The first spirit-photographer was William H. Mumler, a Boston engraver. He developed a self-portrait that featured an apparition of his cousin who had died 12 years earlier. He said, "One Sunday while entirely alone in this gallery I attempted to get a picture of myself, and then it was that I first discovered while developing it that a second form appeared on the plate. At this time I had never heard about spirit pictures, although I had been somewhat interested in the doctrine of Spiritualism. At first I labored under what is now the general impression, that the plate upon which the picture was taken could not have been clean, and that the form which showed itself beside my own must have been left on the glass…"

Mumler became a full-time spirit photographer. His work was analyzed by numerous experts who could not find any evidence that the photos were fraudulent. Still, he was taken to court for fraud, with B.T. Barnum testifying against him. Many came to testify on his behalf, including Mrs. Abraham Lincoln, Mrs. Emma Hardinge Britten, Professor W. D. Gunning, an eminent American geologist, and Moses A. Dow. He was acquitted of fraud, but his reputation was ruined by the event and he never worked in the field again.

Additional Reading for all parts:

Doyle, A.C. (1926) *The History of Spiritualism*, Vol. II, Cassell & Company, London

Kaplan, Louis (2008) *The Strange Case of William Mumler*. University of Minnesota Press

Morse, J.J. (1915) HISTORY OF SPIRIT PHOTOGRAPHY, A Resume, in Three Parts, of the Efforts Made to Obtain Photographs of Departed Persons by Experimenters in Great Britain, the United States, and France from the *Two Worlds,* Friday August 27th

Smithsonian magazine website of the Smithsonian Institution: https://www.smithsonianmag.com/smithsonian-institution/meet-mr-mumler-man-who-captured-lincolns-ghost-camera-180965090/

Spirit Photography: Part II

In 1909, there was an attempt to investigate spirit photography to determine if it was an actual happening or fraud. A commission was set up by the London *Daily Mail* to inquire into the facts of spirit-photography. It consisted of R. Child Bayley, F. J. Mortimer, and E. Sanger-Shepherd, A. P. Sinnett, E. R. Serocold Skeels, and Robert King. Their inquiry was not to conduct experiments, but to evaluate previously produced spirit photographs.

The Commission invited the general public, to send photographs produced under test conditions to the *Daily Mail*. Only a small number were submitted. In the end, the Commission decided that the photographs couldn't be evaluated for the following reasons quoted from their report:

I. That none of the photographs submitted were shown to be taken under conditions which precluded fraud.

II. That photographs submitted by Mr. Sinnett taken in his own presence were clearly the result of "faking" and easily explainable on material grounds.

III. Other photographs shown to us were taken under conditions of which we were told less; but in these we also saw no reason to suppose that anything out of the ordinary played any part. Some of them failed to show anything beyond defects due to careless manipulation, which were mistaken by their producers for supernatural results.

IV. A large proportion of the photographs shown to us which lead any definite spirit-forms on them were produced by one photographer, who appears to be carrying on a business in the production of these things for a profit.

V. According to invitation, packets of plates were sealed by us and submitted to Archdeacon Colley to receive "psychic writing" without being opened. This test, however, was not carried out, as Archdeacon Colley, after receipt of the plates, stated that "his discarnate friend having again recently made progress in the spheres may not from his higher degree yet for a while . . . be able to find the communicating link to transmit through one or more minds removed from this life the faculty or power requisite to impress the photo plate with psychic writing or spirit faces."

VI. A gentleman in Manchester offered to arrange a series of séances with a lady medium at which experiments might be conducted. On the first occasion he was unable to be present. On the second he attended, but informed the Commission that the lady was indisposed, and there was no prospect of the séances being held for a considerable time.

The Commission concluded that unless actual tests could be arranged, they couldn't form an opinion about the photographs. A. P. Sinnett, E. R. Serocold Skeels, and Robert King wrote a column, "The Spiritualist Report" to accompany their decision. They blamed the Commissions failure on the fact that some members "were unacquainted with the intricate science of which spirit-photography is a small part, that it was necessary for them to undertake some preliminary study of Spiritualism generally before they could even appreciate the evidence they might be called upon to deal with." They stated that, "They have shown no inclination to prepare themselves in this way for the work they undertook, nor even to go unprepared in search of the great volume of evidence available. They have merely asked for experimental demonstrations, in ignorance of the conditions under which such demonstrations are possible." They concluded that the "Commission has failed to secure proof that spirit-photography is possible, not because evidence to that effect is otherwise than very abundant, but by reason of the unfortunate and unpractical attitude adopted by those members of the Commission who had no previous experience of the subject."

Even though, the Commission could not come to any conclusion about spirit photography, the conditions under which the photos were taken were documented. The following testimony was given in a letter to Prof. Jas. Coates, of Rothesay, from Mr. John Auld.

"In reply to your expressed wish that I should give you an account of how I obtained the psychic photographs in which you are so much interested, and as you propose to publish my statement, I will be brief.

"In September, 1908, while visiting London, with the object of seeing the Franco- British Exhibition, I embraced the opportunity of calling upon Mr. Boursnell and got my photograph taken, in the hope that some psychic figures might come on the plate. Armed with an introduction given me by Mr. James Robertson, Hon. President of the Glasgow Association of Spiritualists, and with the knowledge that Mr. Boursnell had succeeded in getting many recognised spirit-photographs, I called upon him with some degree of confidence.

"On calling at the house Mr. Boursnell—an old man, who impressed me favourably—met me at the door and escorted me upstairs to a large room, apparently a dining-room, with two windows on one side facing the street. On handing Mr. Boursnell my letter of introduction, I found that he had already given a sitting that day, and that he could not give another to do himself justice. It was arranged that I should call on the following day at noon.

"I was photographed in the room mentioned above. The day was fine and bright outside, and the room was flooded with daylight throughout the sitting. I make this statement definitely, because some critics thought the photos were taken by artificial light. Before taking my photograph, he said there were three psychic forms present in my surroundings, a man and two ladies. He also got the name of "Lizzie."

"In broad daylight he exposed two plates in succession withdrew the slide, and put in a fresh slide, and these were rapidly exposed. I asked him if he thought the figures seen would show on the plates. He told me that they would be there all right. I waited until the plates were developed, when he informed me that there was a spirit-form photographed on each. On receipt of the cabinets I found on two the face of a gentleman about 70 years of age; snow-white hair on head, silvery whiskers, moustache, and beard; expressive eyes, a countenance of much refinement, glowing with intelligence and advanced spirituality. On the other two plates were two ladies, one on each plate. None of the faces were known to me, though the gentleman and one of the ladies are considered by you like those of departed relatives. Mr. James Robertson, who has an extensive collection, and has seen some hundreds of similar photographs, says that they are new to him. Mr. Robertson has obtained through Mr. Boursnell photographs of departed friends under conditions beyond cavil. Mr. Wm. T. Stead and Mr. John Lobb, Editor of "The Christian Age" for over thirty years, have had speaking likenesses of departed friends, and from other sources of testimony, and from my own favourable impressions on seeing Mr. Boursnell, I did not think it necessary to have my photographs taken under test conditions. I trust if Mr. Boursnell is spared, and I have the opportunity of having some further sittings, I hope that I, too, will get a recognisable portrait of some departed friend.

Spirit Photography: Part III

Veteran Spiritualist, Andrew Glendinning, was noted for his investigations into spirit photography. During the period from 1864 to 1908, he experimented in psychic-photography with a number of friends who were mediums. He recorded his experiences with and without the presence of a medium. He published his observations in a book entitled "The Veil Lifted," published in London.

Glendinning related his observations obtained with Mr. James N. Anderson in the presence of Mr. David Duguid, and occasionally with his assistant. They got several pictures, including a portrait of Mr. Anderson's little boy, who had died two years previously. "There he was in the night gown which he had worn on his death-bed, and which had been buried with his lifeless body. Yes, there he was, but with this difference, that his pleasant eyes were now seen open, and instead of the pallor of death, a happy smile was on his face…"

In another instance, Mr. Glendinning relates the story of Mr. John Dewar. Mr. Dewar went to a Mr. Boursnell's hoping to get a picture of his mother. He received instead a portrait of his deceased sister Jeannie who was recognized by relatives and friends. To prevent fraud, Mr. Dewar took his own photographic plates with him. Mr. Boursnell also invited Mr. Dewar to examine the camera and invited both of them into the dark room to develop the plates. Gelndinning said, "I was with them in the dark room during the process of development and fixing. Others have been privileged in the same way when Mr. Boursnell felt certain that they were honest and earnest."

Glendinning also tried capturing spirits without using a camera. In 1892 he found a woman twice on his own plates during the absence of the medium. He noted that there were some differences between the two in the folds of the spirit-drapery. A few days later the same form, with a still different arrangement of drapery was captured on stereoscopic plates by Mr. Jas. Robertson and Glendinning. On that occasion, the medium, Mr. David Duguid, was present.

"Opponents of Spiritualism amuse me by their explanations that I must have procured a statue of 'Clytie,' dressed it with muslin, and photographed it to represent a spirit form," Glendinning said. He insists that was not the case.

Another photograph obtained without the help of a medium, was that of a "foreign-looking" lady on the same plate as himself. He was visited one of his married daughters and had her help expose the plate. The development and fixing was done by Glendinning.

Glendinning also created a series of twenty-six prints without the use of a camera. These were called Dorchagraph's, coined by Andrew Glendinning to distinguish them from thought photography later known as Skotographs. One of them was a portrait of William Haxby. Another portrait was that of Bishop William, of Wykeham, known as the Architect Bishop. "This portrait I obtained several times," Glendinning said. "both with and without the camera, and always exactly the same. This effectually proves that the duplication of the same form with different sitters which sometimes occurs is not by any means a proof of double printing, as has been frequently alleged."

Spirit Photography: Part IV

Thomas Slater was an optical instrument maker in London in the 1840s who, among other things, helped build telescopes. He also had an interest in spiritualism and held meetings at his house. Some of those meetings included Mr. Robert Owen and Lord Brougham. Mr. Owen remarked that when he died, he would return and appear in spirt photographs. After Owen's death, Slater tried his hand at spirit photography and indeed produced a photo with the likeness of Mr. Owen.

Trying to prove to skeptics that spirit photographs were more than illusions produced during the developing process, he decided to study the phenomena. He wrote of his experiences producing photographs with Mr. Fredrick A. Hudson.

At first the two began with normal photography. "He took a negative of me, and it turned out to be a very good one, namely, a clear, sharp negative—nothing more," Slater said. A second photograph was taken with an old plate that had been cleaned. Nothing appeared on that plate when it was developed. During the third attempt, Slater thought of his dead mother while the photograph was taken. "On the plate is a fine female figure, draped in white standing before me with her hand resting on my head," Slater said. "The drapery nearly covers the whole of my body, leaving only the side of the head and one hand visible. I am certain Mr. Hudson played no tricks on this occasion."

Skeptics suggested that the trickery might occur within the camera itself. To disprove that, Mr. Slater made "a new combination of lenses, and took a new camera and several glass plates" to Mr. Hudson's studio. They focused the new camera on a sitter and produced a "fine spirit-picture." This was repeated with another sitter, and with similar success.

Mr. Slater stated that, "Collusion or trickery was altogether out of the question."

Mr. Slater carried on with a further experiment. He created a camera with dark lenses. "The color of the glass was such as only in the strongest light you can see the sitter at all."

"And no one was more astonished than Mr. Hudson, after seeing me focus the instrument to a lady sitting in the chair, to find not only a sharp, well-defined negative with good half-tone, but also that standing by the lady was a fine spirit-figure, draped in black and white," Mr. Slater said.

He asked skeptics to explain why they were able to take portraits of persons through instruments that excluded so much light that the sitter was scarcely visible. At the same time, the spirits were impressed vividly upon the photographic plates. He said, "I am now carrying on experiments upon this part of the spectrum, and am convinced that much may and will be discovered that is useful in photography by making use of invisible light."

The Scole Experiment

Even though physical mediumship began in the 19th century, it wasn't until near the end of the 20th century before any long term experimental type investigation was conducted. The Scole Experiment took place between 1993 and 1998 and was led by four core members, Robin and Sandra Foy and Alan and Diana Bylett who were experienced mediums. The trials took place in the cellar of Foy's 17th century farmhouse located in the village of Scole in northeast England.

The cellar room was about 15 x 30 feet and painted midnight blue. The four would sit around a circular wooden table which held various crystals. All sessions were conducted in complete darkness and participants wore luminous armbands, so all could observe their movements.

According to Robin Foy, "What we wanted to do was to provide physical evidence for other people to witness, which would provide actual proof of life after death that could be studied scientifically. In short we wanted to prove beyond any doubt that life goes on beyond death."

Although the four were experienced mediums, it took meeting twice a week for a year before any results were observed. In October 1993, they witnessed the first of a series of paranormal phenomena, a coin was 'apported' out of thin air and materialized on the table.

After that, they witnessed a variety of lights darting around the room. Objects levitated and floated. Voices emanated from mid-air. This was followed by two-way communications with a team of spirit people through a cheap tape recorder.

The four were informed by spirit entities that the location of the house was a significant factor in helping build a bridge between the worlds. The ability to create this bridge was assisted by what they referred to as 'creative energy.'

Over time there was a remarkable range of physical evidence produced, including photographic and video material, numerous apports, levitating of objects, spirit hands interacting with observers and spirit voices communicating directly from a point in space.

One apport was a pristine copy of the Daily Mail dated April 1, 1944 that included an article about medium Helen Duncan's 18-month prison sentence which was handed down under the Witchcraft Act. The paper was found to be genuine and in such excellent condition it would have had to have been in special protective storage for 50 years.

Scientific observers, including David Fontana, Arthur Ellison and Montague Keen, were invited to monitor sessions as well as a professional magician. The highly respected Society for Psychical Research in London conducted a lengthy investigation and published a positive report.

Additional reading:

Scole Website: www.thescoleexperiment.com

Section III:

NOTABLE PEOPLE

Mother Leafy Anderson: African American Medium

There is no birth record for Leafy Anderson, but her obituary said she was born in 1887 in Balboa, Wisconsin, a town that never existed. Wherever she was born, she eventually moved to Louisiana and married William Anderson in Raceland. That marriage did not last. Anderson left her husband and moved to Chicago in 1914 before relocating to New Orleans in 1918.

The Spiritualist movement spread quickly throughout America during the 1920s. Because of segregation laws, in 1922 the National Spiritualist Association of Churches expelled its Black members. This led to the formation of the Colored Spiritualist Association of Churches. Within a few years there were Black Spiritualist churches located in Chicago, Detroit, Philadelphia, and many other cities.

Most churches in the 1920s were led by male pastors. Anderson broke that mold. She founded the Spiritualist movement in New Orleans. Her church included the use of Spirit Guides in worship services along with a mixture of Protestant and Catholic practices.

Anderson trained other women to assume leadership roles as the movement spread across the city. She invited jazz bands to play in her church when many black ministers denounced it as the devil's music. New Orleans churches later dropped the "ist" from their name and called themselves Spiritual, putting a greater emphasis on Jesus.

Anderson taught followers to summon spirits, offering classes for a dollar a session. She was known for her yellow and gold robes draped with a mantel bearing the image of Black Hawk, her spirit guide. She told her followers that she had found the spirit of Black Hawk, an historical person, in Chicago. She considered him a protective figure and guardian who united the beliefs of Christianity with the ancient idea of a spiritual cosmology.

Anderson died of flu in 1927. Her last words, reportedly, were, "I am going away, and I am coming back, but you shall know that I am here."

After her death, Anderson's successor, Mother Catherine Seals, ran The Temple of the Innocent Blood church. When Seals died, the church broke apart, giving rise to many Spiritualist denominations in New Orleans and elsewhere.

Additional Reading:

http://www.academia.edu/5823629/Leafy_Anderson_and_the_Success_of_Black_Spiritualism_in_New_Orleans

Baer, Hans A., and Merrill Singer (1992) African-American Religion in the Twentieth Century: Varieties of Protest and Accommodation. Knoxville: University of Tennessee Press

Jacobs, Claude F., and Andrew F. Kaslow (1991) The Spiritual Churches of New Orleans: Origins, Beliefs, and Rituals of an African-American Religion. Knoxville: University of Tennessee Press

Albert (Wishart) Best: Trance Medium

Albert Wishart was a native of Belfast, Ireland. Born to a teenaged mother in October 1917, he was informally adopted by the Best family soon after. Albert did not speak much about his childhood, only mentioning that it was difficult. Although modest and reclusive, he was known for his sense of humor, his love of whiskey, and friendly personality.

Albert recalled having his first spiritual experience at the age of seven in 1925, when he saw the full materialization of a discarnate Spirit. That same year, the Belfast Spiritualist Alliance was established at Central Hall, near his home. The Alliance would later play a pivotal role in Albert's development.

Albert quit school at the age of 14 after Mrs. Best died. In 1932, he began working as a fitter in the Belfast Rope Works. He also attended the Belfast Spiritualist Alliance Church. It wasn't long before they recognized Albert's spiritual gifts. He was invited to sit in a circle for development.

Albert married, and he and Rose had three children. September 1939, he volunteered to join the 6th Battalion of the Royal Inniskillen Fusiliers. He was taken prisoner of war and shot twice; once in the mouth and once in his left hand, which left it paralyzed. After being released from prison camp, he returned home to find that Rose and the children had been killed during a German air raid in Belfast on May 5, 1941. What remained of the bodies was buried in a mass grave.

Albert was devastated and wouldn't return to Belfast permanently. Instead, he moved to Scotland and settled in Ayrshire where we worked for the Post Office. He found a development circle there, and by 1951 started to attend the

Spiritualist Church in Kilmarnock. Utilizing his experience in the Post Office, he was not only able to give the names of visiting spirits during trance, he could also give addresses and telephone numbers as well as information about past lives and events.

One person witnessed the following during one of Best's demonstrations: "If I had not been in the company of people who I consider sane of mind, I would not have believed my eyes, as the chair, along with Mr. Best, lifted up till the little man's head was near ceiling height. No sooner had this happened than voices could be heard, which I can say came from no one seen sitting in that room. The chair slowly returned to the floor with Mr. Best still calling out to the invisible forces around him and the session ended soon after. The medium explained that he was unharmed and never in any danger, but he did not like it when they played games like that just to impress people. He said that the spirits who had played this prank on him were men who had been part of his squadron during the war and who had died in Africa in 1943. This was Mr. Best's account; quite honestly, I, along with the most of my group, even those among us with a background in physics, have absolutely no explanation for what we experienced."

By the late 1950's, Albert left his job in the Post Office and moved to Glasgow. He joined a new healing sanctuary in Thornhill and remained as a Healer in this non-denominational sanctuary until 1982. Albert traveled the world, visiting places like India and Australia. On his visit to India in 1991, he warned Prime Minister Rajiv Gandhi to stay out of crowds as he was in great peril. Weeks later, Gandhi was assassinated by a suicide bomber. He also saw the materialization of his children while visiting India. Both his mediumship and healing ability were legendary.

Albert turned down countless offers to appear on television but mentored celebrity mediums Colin Fry and Gordon Smith. He was a renowned tutor at Arthur Findlay College for years. He was honored for his unceasing work for Spiritualism by being awarded Spiritualist of the Year in 1994.

Albert was taken into Hospital in Glasgow on April, 2 1996. At one point he saw his wife and children in the room with him. Witnesses said there were tears of joy in his eyes, and he told visitors: 'They've come, you will have to let me go." Afterward, he slipped into a coma from which he never regained full consciousness. He passed ten days later and left his body to medical research with a Scottish University. Best is considered one of the most important Spiritualist Mediums of the 21st Century.

Additional Reading:

Flood, Michael R. (2015) Out of the Medium's Mouth: Spiritualism in Ireland. ASSMPI

https://theothersidepress.com/albert-best-the-man-the-medium-3187

Helena Blavatsky: The Theosophical Society

Blavatsky was born in Ekaterinoslav, Russia in 1831, the daughter of Colonel Peter von Hahn and Helena de Fadeyev, a renowned novelist. At an early age, she was gifted as a linguist, pianist, artist, and naturalist. She also possessed psychic powers that puzzled her family and friends.

She married the middle-aged Nikifor V. Blavatsky, Vice-Governor of the Province of Yerivan when she was 17. The marriage was never consummated. After few months, she escaped and travelled to Turkey, Egypt, and Greece.

While in London in 1851, Blavatsky said she met Mahatma Morya. He informed her that she was destined for special work, and she accepted his guidance from that point onward. Her travels took her to North and South America, the West Indies, and Japan. While visiting Tibet, she was able to acquire some of her occult training with Master Morya. She then traveled to Russia for a time and visited the Balkans, Greece, Egypt, Syria and Italy and other countries. She returned to Tibet in 1868 and met Master Koot Hoomi for the first time. She said she stayed in his house in Little Tibet and studied clairvoyance, clairaudience and telepathy.

Blavatsky joined the Spiritualist movement in the early 1870s, but didn't believe that the entities contacted were the spirits of the dead. In 1874, she met Colonel Henry Steel Olcott, who had served in the U.S. Government and was practicing law in New York. She was also introduced to William Quan Judge, a young Irish lawyer. The three of them along with other friends, founded The Theosophical Society in 1875. The society's purpose was to "promulgate the ancient teachings of Theosophy, or the Wisdom concerning the Divine, which had been the spiritual basis of other great movements of the past, such as Neo-Platonism, Gnosticism, and the Mystery-Schools of the Classical world."

Blavatsky's first book, *Isis Unveiled*, "outlined the history, scope and development of the Occult Sciences, the nature and origin of Magic, the roots of Christianity, the errors of Christian Theology and the fallacies of established orthodox Science."

They established their Theosophical Headquarters and their first journal in Bombay in 1879. Although opposed by the British government, Theosophy spread rapidly in India. It was not without problems. Blavatsky was accused of creating fraudulent paranormal phenomena. She remained a controversial figure during her lifetime, championed by supporters and derided as a fraudulent charlatan and plagiarist by critics.

In ill health, Blavatsky pushed onward. She wrote her second work, *The Secret Doctrine*, in 1884. Volume I concentrated on the evolution of the universe. Volume II discussed the evolution of humanity. In 1888 she formed the Esoteric Section of the Theosophical Society for the deeper study of the Esoteric Philosophy by dedicated students. In 1890, she established the European Headquarters of the society in London.

After completing two more books, Blavatsky died in London in 1891 during a flu epidemic.

Additional Reading:

Blavatsky Website: http://www.blavatsky.net/

Mina (Margery) Crandon: Physical Medium

Mina Stinson was born in 1888 in Ontario, Canada. She moved to Boston at the age of 17 where, after an unsuccessful first marriage, she met Dr. LeRoi Godard Crandon, a successful surgeon. They married in in 1918 and she became well established in the Boston social scene.

Dr. Crandon became interested in Spiritualism and psychic research in 1923 and invited friends to his home to try a table tilting séance. The table began to move, slightly at first, but then more violently. Wanting to know which guest possessed the psychic talent needed to cause the action, Dr. Crandon instructed the guests to remove their hands from the table, one by one. He discovered that the medium was his own wife.

It was only a few months later that Mina discovered that Walter Stinson, her brother who was killed in a train crash in 1911, was communicating to her from the Spirit World. Soon, Walter was able to speak directly through Mina, often using colorful language.

Mina's talent developed rapidly. She levitated tables and created other forms of physical phenomenon. Attendance at her séances became by invitation only and she soon attracted the attention of researchers.

The first formal investigation conducted by a committee from Harvard, arranged by Professor William McDougal, head of Harvard's Department of Psychology. After five months of observation the committee decided that a majority of the telekinetic phenomena was fraudulently produced but gave no opinion on the trance communication.

Refusing to accept the committee conclusions, Dr. Crandon took Mina to Europe for more tests. Sir Arthur Conan Doyle declared her be a very powerful medium.

In 1922, the Scientific American offered $2,500 to anyone who could provide conclusive evidence of physical paranormal phenomena. The judging committee was to include Harry Houdini, but he wasn't notified when the investigation began in January 1924. When he learned about the trials three months later, the committee was about to declare Crandon genuine.

Houdini was furious. He traveled to Boston and discovered the committee was staying at Crandon's home. He felt this had compromised their objectivity. Houdini constructed a cabinet with steel bolts and padlocks and defied her to produce any paranormal phenomena. The cabinet was small and hot, but Crandon agree to sit inside. No physical effects were produced, and Walter accused Houdini of planting something in the cabinet to frame her.

After the cabinet was opened, a collapsible ruler was discovered on the floor. Houdini accused her of using the ruler with her mouth to try to produce physical phenomena. Harry Houdini took credit for exposing her as a fraud.

Everyone thought that was the end of the story until William Lindsay Gresham published a book which included an account given by Jim Collins, Houdini's assistant. Collins admitted that he had planted the ruler in the cabinet to discredit Crandon.

Despite the failure with Houdini, Crandon continued to produce psychic breezes, raps, trance, trance writings, independent voice communication, apportations, paraffin gloves and fingerprints. She was probably the most tested medium of the 1920's, examined by Dr. Joseph Rhine and the American Society for Psychical Research. Each concluded that the physical manifestations were fraudulently produced. She was never able to prove conclusively that he was a real medium.

Additional Reading:

http://www.prairieghosts.com/margery.html

Neher, Andrew (2011). Paranormal and Transcendental Experience: A Psychological Examination. Dover reprint edition.

Tietze, Thomas (1973). *Margery*. Harper & Row Publishers.

Emma Hardinge Britten and the Seven Principles

Emma was born in London in 1823 as Emma Floyd. She developed a reputation as a psychic medium very early. As a child, she predicted people's futures and spoke about their deceased relatives, of whom she had no prior knowledge. When her father died in 1834, she began to support herself and her family, working as a musician, and opera singer. According to her autobiography, Emma joined a secret London occult society which used different clairvoyant techniques for experimental purposes. It is suspected that she received the name Hardinge from this society.

Emma came to America in the hopes of testing American susceptibility to Spiritualism. Instead, she witnessed many mystical experiences at séances that led her to becoming a part of the Spiritualist movement. She hosted spiritualist séances at the Society for the Diffusion of Spiritual Knowledge, worked as a "trance lecturer" and delivered speeches across the country.

Hardinge also became politically active in 1864, supporting Abraham Lincoln's re-election. After delivering a lecture entitled, "The Coming Man; or the Next President of the United States," she went on a thirty-two-lecture tour.

Emma married Spiritualist, William Britten, in 1870, the same year her book, *Modern American Spiritualism* was published. In 1872, she attempted to start a magazine, *The Western Star*, but it failed after six issues were published.

Today, Emma is most known for her addition of the Seven Principles to the Spiritualist movement. In her autobiography, edited by Emma's sister, Margaret Wilkinson, she wrote of the event where the principles were first suggested.

Margaret and Emma were well acquainted with the Fox sisters, who were known for their communication with spirits through knocking sounds. The eldest sister, Mrs. Leah Underhill, was one of the best rapping and physical mediums that they had ever met. Emma said that Leah, "never flagged in her devotion to the cause she had espoused, but opened her handsome house in 37th Street, New York, for winter evening receptions, in which, whenever I was in the city, she kindly invited me to become her associate."

At one séance attended by Emma Hardinge and her mother, Oliver and Mary Anne Johnson, Robert Dale Owen, William Lloyd Garrison, and a few others, the spirit of Robert Owen manifested with loud rappings and calls for the alphabet. He communicated that "he wished to give a set of Spiritual Commandments through Emma, if she would kindly submit to his control, whilst his son, Robert Dale Owen, should transcribe them as the entranced medium spoke."

The Ten Spiritual Commandments dictated were:

I. Thou shalt search for truth in every department of being: Test, prove, and try if what thou deemest truth is truth, and then accept it as the word of God.

II. Thou shalt continue the search for truth all thy life: And never cease to test, prove, and try all that thou deemest to be truth.

III. Thou shalt search by every attainable means for the laws that underlie all life and being: Thou shalt strive to comprehend these laws, live in harmony with them, and make them the laws of thine own life, thy rule and guide in all thine actions.

IV. Thou shalt not follow the example of any man or set of men: Nor obey any teaching or accept of any theory as thy rule of life that is not in strict accordance with thy highest sense of right.

V. Thou shalt remember that a wrong done to the least of thy fellow creatures is a wrong done to all: And thou shalt never commit a wrong wilfully and consciously to any of thy fellow-men, nor connive at wrong done by others without striving to prevent or protesting against it.

VI. Thou shalt acknowledge all men's rights to do, think, or speak, to be exactly equal to thine own: And all rights whatsoever that thou dost demand thou shalt ever accord to others.

VII. Thou shalt not hold thyself bound to love, or associate with those that are distasteful or repulsive to thee: But thou shalt be held bound to treat such objects of dislike with gentleness, courtesy, and justice, and never suffer thine antipathies to make thee ungentle or unjust to any living creature.

VIII. Thou shalt ever regard the rights, interests, and welfare of the many as superior to those of the one or the few: And in cases where thy welfare, or that of thy friend, is to be balanced against that of society, thou shalt sacrifice thyself, or friend, to the welfare of the many.

IX. Thou shalt be obedient to the laws of the land in which thou dost reside: In all things which do not conflict with thy highest sense of right.

X. Thy first and last duty upon earth, and all through thy life, shall be to seek for the principles of right, and to live them out to the utmost of thy power: And whatever creed, precept, or example conflicts with those principles, thou shalt shun and reject, ever remembering that the laws of right are - in morals, JUSTICE; in science, HARMONY; in religion, THE FATHERHOOD OF GOD, THE BROTHERHOOD OF MAN, the immortality of the human soul, and compensation and retribution for the good or evil done on earth.

These first principles, which were first dictated in 1871, were discussed and altered over time until they eventually became the Seven Principles of Spiritualism in 1887.

Additional Reading:

Wilkinson, Margaret (1900) *Autobiography of Emma Hardinge Britten*, Posthumously edited and published by her sister. Spiritualists National Union (reprinted 1996)

Gaunt, Paul J. The Creed of the Spirits. Spiritualist National Union

Sir Arthur Conan Doyle: Author and Spiritualist

Sir Arthur Conan Doyle was born in Edinburgh Scotland in 1859. Conan Doyle's father died when he was very young, and his wealthy uncles sent him to a Jesuit preparatory school. From 1876 to 1881, he studied medicine at the University of Edinburgh Medical School. It was during his medical training that he began to write short fiction stories, which eventually led to his Sherlock Holmes tales.

Conan Doyle married twice. His first wife, Louise Hawkins died of tuberculosis, leaving behind two children, Mary and Kingsley. Conan Doyle married his second wife, Jean Leckie, in 1906. They had three children.

Conan Doyle volunteered as a doctor during the Boer War. Afterward, he became interested in Spiritualism. Although skeptical, he followed all the recent research and even attended some séances. His skepticism was pushed aside during World War I, when he had to face the death of relatives and friends.

The event that convinced Conan Doyle of Spiritualism's authenticity was his meeting with Lily Lauder-Symonds. Conan Doyle's brother-in-law and good friend, Malcom Leckie, was killed in World War I in 1916. Leckie had previously given Conan Doyle a guinea coin, saying that it was his first fee payment as an Army doctor. Conan Doyle wore it fondly on his watch chain but never spoke of it. When Lauder-Symonds mentioned the coin during her reading, he knew she had contacted the spirit of Malcom Leckie.

Conan Doyle put aside his fiction writing and began lecturing on Spiritualism in 1917. He traveled the world attending séances and debating the topic. In 1919, magician P.T. Selbit staged a séance, but Conan Doyle said to the press, "I should have to see it again before passing a definite opinion on it," and: "I have my doubts about the whole thing." In 1920, Doyle debated notable sceptic Joseph McCabe in London, McCabe insisting that Conan Doyle was being duped.

Conan Doyle travelled to Australia and New Zealand as a Spiritualist missionary in 1920, and continued speaking about his Spiritualist convictions in Britain, Europe, and the United States. He wrote many non-fictional Spiritualist works, including a popular book, *The Coming of Fairies* in 1922, and two volumes on the history of spiritualism.

Conan Doyle became friends with Harry Houdini, who was a prominent opponent of Spiritualism. He even insisted that Houdini used special psychic gifts to aide his magical tricks. Their opposing views eventually led to the severing of the friendship. Conan Doyle continued to support Spiritualism until he died in 1930.

Additional Reading:

http://www.arthurconandoyle.com/

Doyle, Arthur C. (1921) *The Wanderings of a Spiritualist*. Hodder & Stoughton. Reprinted 2018 by Forgotten Books.

Andrew Jackson Davis: The Poughkeepsie Seer

Most attribute the beginnings of Spiritualism to the Fox sisters from Hydesville, New York. Their communication with a spirit through rappings lead to an investigation into the afterlife. But the Fox sisters' communications were not an isolated incident. Years before their experiences in their rural cabin, Andrew Jackson Davis was not only obtaining information visiting the Spirit World while in a trance state, he predicted the rise of Spiritualism.

Andrew Jackson Davis was born in Blooming Grove, a small town along the Hudson River. The family moved frequently, and Davis received little education. He eventually apprenticed to a shoemaker for two years and would have run a typical business if he hadn't attended a lecture on Animal Magnetism given by Dr. J.S. Grimes in Poughkeepsie, New York.

Davis tried the hypnotic technique but didn't have any success with it until a local tailor, William Livingston, threw him into a trance. In the trance state, he reached a higher plane of consciousness. While on this plane, he could understand the laws of the universe. He diagnosed and prescribed cures for individuals and explained spiritual and metaphysical phenomena.

Even though he only had 5 months schooling and claimed to have read only a handful of books, he dictated a book in 1846 entitled, *Principles of Nature*. It was published a year later when he was only 21. He eventually published over 30 books with topics that included the seven planes of existence, health, science, philosophy, and education. In the *Great Harmonia*, he refers to evolution nine years before Darwin published his book, *On the Origin of Species*. He also predicted the existence of the planets Neptune and Pluto before their discovery.

Davis predicted the coming of Spiritualism in *Principles of Nature* (1847), saying, "And the world will hail with delight the ushering in of that era when the interiors of men will be opened, and the spiritual communion will be established." The Fox family would have their encounter with their famous rapping spirit just a year later.

Several sources during the time mentioned that Davis met with President Abraham Lincoln, both at the Whitehouse and in Davis' home in New York. Davis eventually obtained a medical degree and moved to Boston where he opened a book shop and prescribed herbal remedies. He died in 1910.

Additional Reading:

http://www.ascsi.org/ASCS/Library/LegacyRoom/Biographies/Davis_AJ.pdf

DeSalvo, John (2006) Andrew Jackson Davis-The First American Prophet and Clairvoyant. LuLu.com

Leslie Flint: Direct Voice Medium

Leslie Flint was born in London in 1910. At the age of eight, he saw the apparition of a deceased uncle in his grandmother's kitchen. Around the same time, he became aware that the voices whispering all round him were not of this world.

Flint worked as a cemetery gardener, grave-digger, a semi-professional dancer, a cinema usher and a barman before he attempted mediumship. He founded a spiritualist circle in Sydney Grove, Hendon, to demonstrate his psychic gifts and prove the spirit-transcended existence of the physical body. He conducted his first séance at the age of 17. His first public séance was held in 1955 for an association he had formed called the Temple of Light.

Flint had a spirit guide named Mickey, who was a child killed in 1910. But his connection was not limited to Mickey. An avid fan of Rudolph Valentino, he made repeated contact with the spirit of the man as well as other notable persons. But most of the spirit voices were of ordinary people, sending messages of hope and comfort to those attending his demonstrations.

Flint didn't use trumpets or other paraphernalia. While sitting in total darkness, he worked wide awake, not in a trance. During séances, people reported hearing voices from around the room. They could respond to kin, strangers and famous individuals who manifested around Flint. Despite his gaining popularity, he never charged for his séances.

In the mid-1930s, Flint was filling the biggest halls in London and answering mailbags of letters. He submitted to a variety of tests to disprove accusations of ventriloquism or other deceptions. In one séance, he held a measured quantity of colored water in his mouth during the demonstration. A throat microphone was used to register vibrations from his larynx while the voices spoke during another gathering. Flint said, "I have been boxed up, tied up, sealed up, gagged, bound and held - and still the voices have come to speak their message of life eternal…"

Flint eventually allowed anyone to tape-record his séances. Recordings are now stored at the University of Manitoba. About 2,000 audiotapes and 300 books make up the collection.

As Flint aged, bronchitis and other health problems took their toll. His abilities became unreliable and the voices faded. He died in May of 1994.

Additional reading:

http://www.leslieflint.com

Harry Edwards: Spiritual Healer

Harry Edwards was born in London in 1893, the son of a printer and one of nine children. In 1907 he left school to begin a seven-year apprenticeship to become printer but was dissatisfied with the career. He became active in politics, but when World War I broke out, he enlisted in the Royal Sussex Regiment. He returned to England in 1921, married and had four children. He and his wife, Phyllis, opened a stationer's shop and printing works to support the family. Edwards tried to launch himself into a political career but had no success.

Edwards had no interest in spiritual healing until he attended a meeting at a Spiritualist Church in 1936. He was told by the mediums that he had healing powers. Encouraged by them, he practiced as a healer while running the printing business. His healings were so successful that his reputation spread. With the outbreak of the Second World War, Harry joined the Home Guard and provided healing to members of the Armed Forces and even his own son. His healing sessions continued, despite the bombing of his house and the loss of all his distant healing patients' records. After the war his fame spread. The family moved to Stoneleigh in Surry and he opened a healing sanctuary in his home.

Edwards claimed that several scientists worked through him, including Lord Lister and Louis Pasteur. The number of people seeking healing increased and Edwards could no longer accommodate them in his small home. In 1946, the family moved into a larger house in Burrows Lea. The house sat on several acres and he eventually created the Harry Edwards Healing Sanctuary. By that point, he was receiving 10,000 letters a week and conducting distance healing.

During the 1940s and 50s, Edwards drew crowds of thousands to his healing demonstrations. In 1955 he founded and was the first President of the National Federation of Spiritual Healers. When the Archbishops' Commission on Divine Healing was set up in 1953, Edwards addressed the Commission, providing it with documented evidence of a number of successful healings. The Commission's report rejected any claims of spiritual healing. A study in the British Medical Journal by Rose in 1954 could not verify any of Edwards healing claims.

The reputation of Harry Edwards and Spiritual Healing continued to grow and vast numbers of people from all over the world continued to contact the Sanctuary. Harry Edwards died in December 1976 aged 83.

Additional Reading:

Harry Edwards Website:

https://www.harryedwardshealingsanctuary.org.uk/

Geoffrey Hodson: Angels, Spirits and Fairies.

Geoffrey Hodson was born in Lincolnshire, England in 1886. During his boyhood, he had several psychic experiences. It was during that time that he was contacted by a spirit which he would later identify as a Kundalini life force known as the Serpent Fire. In his early twenties, he studied spiritualism, but it was not the philosophy of life he was seeking. It wasn't until he attended a lecture by Dr. Annie Besant in Manchester in 1912, that he found and joined the Theosophical Society.

World War I interrupted his search for the truth. He joined the Tank Corps as a Commander and was dispatched to France and Belgium in 1918. After the war, he married Jane Carter and joined the YMCA Secretariat. It was around this time he met Mrs. Mary De La Middleton who said that her spirit guide had instructed her to show Hodson how to awaken his abilities.

Hodson worked on his meditation skills and study of theosophy. He and Jane toured Lancashire on his motorcycle, making detailed notes on the various types of fairies and nature spirits Hodson perceived in each location. When they reached the valley of Sheepscombe, he was contacted by an angel named Bethelda and began working with higher spirits.

Seven orders of angels are mentioned in The Bible, but Hodson said there are many more. They act as "creative and directive intelligence behind various universal qualities such as love, music, power etc." Instead of angel, which means messenger, he used the word "deva," which is the Sanskrit term for celestial or shining being, when describing them.

Hodson travelled around the world three times while lecturing for the Theosophical Society. His contact with Bethelda led to his meeting angels and other spiritual beings in every country that he visited. He said they recognized him as an "Ambassador between the Human and the Angelic Kingdom." They offered their assistance and aided his investigations. On one occasion they helped with his healing work, curing not only those who came to him, but also renewing his own energy.

He considered fairies as "junior members" of the angelic kingdom. Although many thought fairies were mere fantasy, he figured they were so prevalent in fables of every country that they shouldn't be disregarded. He described the appearance and function of nature spirits in his early books, *Fairies at Work and at Play* (1925) and *The Kingdom of Faerie* (1927). He was privileged to meet with the Maori Princess Te Puea, who also possessed certain mystical abilities. She taught him about the race of fairies known to the Maori as the Patupaiarehe in New Zealand.

Over his lifetime, Hodson wrote over 50 books on a variety of subjects and hundreds of articles about his investigations and the angelic teachings given to him throughout his life.

After spending long periods of his time in Australia and New Zealand, he eventually settled in Auckland and became a naturalized New Zealand Citizen. His last lecture was given when he was 96 years old, eight months before his death in 1983.

Additional Reading:

Geoffrey Hodson Website: http://www.geoffreyhodson.com

Allan Kardec: Father of Spiritism

Spiritism is defined as "a progressive body of knowledge which studies the nature, origin and destiny of Spirits as well as their physical relationship to the world."

Allan Kardec was born Léon-Dénizarth-Hippolyte Rivail at Lyons in 1804, the member of an old family of Bourg-en-Bresse. His father and grandfather were barristers of good standing and high character. Kardec was educated at the Institution of Pestalozzi, at Yverdun (Canton de Vaud). He had a passion for teaching and devoted himself to helping his fellow students by the age of 14. He was most interested in botany and spent much of his time in the mountains in search of specimens for his herbarium.

After finishing at Yverdun, he returned to Lyons. Instead of pursuing law, he purchased a school for boys where he offered courses in Chemistry, Physics, Anatomy and Astronomy. He published many educational books in the 1830s and 40s and was a member of several learned societies.

His interest in science lead to investigations into magnetism, trance, clairvoyance and other psychic phenomena. When table-turning became popular in the 1850s, he became interested in the nature of "spiritist" phenomena. A friend of his had two daughters who were mediums. Usually their messages were gay and lively. But when Kardec attended their séances, the conversation grew serious. He was told that "spirits of a much higher order than those who habitually communicated through the two young mediums came expressly for him, and would continue to do so, in order to enable him to fulfill an important religious mission."

He asked the mediums to meet with him twice a week, so he could question the spirits. The girls consented and brought forth answers from the spirit world through table-rapping and planchette-writing. The replies, which were little understood by the mediums, continued for two years and became the basis for Kardec's spiritist theory.

Kardec said to his wife, "It is a most curious thing! My conversations with the invisible intelligences have completely revolutionized my ideas and convictions."

The spirits instructed him to write a book and publish under the pseudonym, Allan Kardec. It was entitled: *Le Livre des Esprits (The Spirits' Book)*. When published in 1857, it became very popular, making converts not only in France, but all over the Continent. The name of Allan Kardec became a household word.

Soon after its publication, he founded The Parisian Society of Psychologic Studies for the purpose of obtaining instructions through mediums to elucidate truth and duty. He also founded and edited a monthly magazine, entitled *La Revue Spirite, Journal of Psychologic Studies*. Similar associations were soon formed all over the world. Many of these published periodicals in support of the new doctrine, and all of them transmitted to the Parisian Society the most remarkable of the spirit-communications received by them.

From the materials furnished to him from around the globe, he enlarged and completed *The Spirits' Book*, Revised Edition in 1857. Kardec himself would go on to edit and publish four other books through this cooperation with the spirit world before passing in 1869: *The Mediums' Book* (1861), *The Gospel According to Spiritism* (1864), *Heaven and Hell* (1865), and *The Genesis* (1868).

Thousands visited Kardec, including many of high rank in the social, literary, artistic, and scientific worlds. The Emperor

Napoleon III., who was interested in spiritist-phenomena, sent for him several times to discuss his book.

Suffering from heart disease, in 1869 Allan Kardec drew up the plan of a new spiritist organization that would carry on the work after his death. To this society, which was to be called The Joint Stock Company for the Continuation of the Works of Allan Kardec, he intended to bequeath the copyright of his spiritist writings and of the *Revue Spirite*.

On the 31st of March 1869, after he finished drawing up the constitution and rules of the society, he was seated in his usual chair at his study-table. His quickly passed from the earth to the spirit-world.

Additional Reading:

Allan Kardec Website: http://spiritisthouston.org/who-we-are/who-was-allan-kardec/

Helen Keller: Swedenborg Follower

Helen Keller was born in Tuscumbia, Alabama in 1880. For her first year and a half, she was like any other child. However, at nineteen months, she became ill with "brain fever," which may have been scarlet fever or meningitis. Helen survived the serious illness but had been left blind and deaf. Helen described her early years as filled with nothing except "the instinct to eat and drink and sleep." Her days were "a blank without past, present, or future, without hope or anticipation, without interest or joy."

She described her contact with Anne Mansfield Sullivan as a transition from "nothingness to human life." Anne arrived at their Alabama home in March of 1887 and became Helen's personal tutor. Helen described her realization that the sign Anne was creating on her palm represented water was her first revelation. "It was as if I had come back to life after being dead!"

Helen eventually attended the Perkins School in Boston. It was there that she was introduced to John Hitz, whom she befriended until his death sixteen years later. John brought the religious writings of eighteenth century Swedish scientist and seer, Emanuel Swedenborg, to Helen's attention when he gave her a copy of his book, *Heaven and Hell*.

Even though Helen's father was a deacon in the Presbyterian church and her mother an Episcopalian, Helen was baptized but received no special religious training. She described Swedenborg's book as a second revelation. "My heart gave a joyous bound," she said. 'Here was a faith that emphasized what I felt so keenly—the separateness between soul and body, between the realm I could picture as a whole, and the chaos of fragmentary things and irrational contingencies that my limited senses met at every turn." She credited Swedenborg with giving her a faith that turned her darkness into light. "I believe in the immortality of the soul because I have within me immortal longings. I believe that the state we enter after death is wrought of our own motives, thoughts, and deeds."

Helen devoted her life to service, not only helping those confronted with blindness or deafness, but working to end ignorance, racism and poverty. She supported the right of workers to strike and women to vote and was the first woman to receive an honorary degree from Harvard.

She saw this new type of belief, not as a matter of doctrine, but as a loving way to understand the world. In 1928, she addressed the national meeting of Swedenborgians in Washington, DC. Her vision of Christianity was universal and all-encompassing. She saw that Swedenborgian ideals fostered true freedom and placed humanity above party, country and race. She said, "I believe that life is given us so that we may grow in love, and I believe that God is in me as the sun is in the color and fragrance of a flower-the Light in my darkness, the Voice in my silence."

Additional Reading:

Keller, Helen (1927) *Light in My Darkness*. Reprinted 2000, Chrysalis Books, editor Ray Silverman

Robert James Lees: Boy Medium

Robert James Lees was born in Hinkley, England in 1849. He claimed to have had his first psychic experience at the age of three. He saw a mysterious kilted Highlander when he was alone in his room, unable to sleep in the dark. The man talked and sang to him until he fell asleep.

Prince Albert died in 1861. Lees was only 13-year-old at the time, but he went into trance and communicated messages from Albert to Queen Victoria. Lees said he lived in Buckingham Palace for short time afterward so that the Queen could regularly talk to Albert through him. By the age of fourteen, Lees was a well-known trance medium, and was called 'boy medium' in and around Birmingham.

In 1871, Lees married Sarah Ann Bishop. They had sixteen children, ten of whom survived. Lees worked as a journalist for the Manchester Guardian, Fleet Street, and other London based publications. He had little formal education but wrote a series of spiritualist books which he said were dictated to him by friends from the spirit realm. His best-known work is the three-volume series entitled *The Mists Trilogy*, written between 1898 – 1931. A copy of the set was received by Queen Victoria.

During the Jack the Ripper murders in 1888, Lees was living in the London area. His diary entries state that in October of that year he went to both the City of London Police and Scotland Yard offer his assistance. He was turned away as a madman on both occasions, though Scotland Yard offered to correspond with him.

Over the years, Lees participation in the Ripper story became greatly exaggerated. A *Chicago Herald* story claimed that he was continually troubled by psychic visions of Jack the Ripper murdering his victims. The same story was perpetuated in an article in *The People* in 1895. Numerous articles and books followed, stating that Lees used his psychic powers to track down the Ripper and help detain him. The police denied that Lees was involved with the Ripper hunt. Lees' own diary entries contradict the published tale.

Despite his lack of involvement with the Ripper case, Lees was a Spiritualist, preacher, writer and healer. In 1902, the family moved to Ilfracombe in Devon. They lived there until about 1928, when he returned to Leicester, where he died in 1931 at the age of 81 years.

Additional Reading:

http://www.casebook.org/dissertations/ripperoo-lees.html

J. Hewat McKenzie: Parapsychology Researcher

J.Hewat McKenzie was born in Edinburgh, Scotland in 1869. He gave up his practice as a psychologist and psychoanalyst in 1900 to pursue his interest in parapsychology. He spent 15 years studying hypnotists and mediums from around the globe. When he returned to England in 1920, he founded the British College of Psychic Science in London with his wife. In 1938, the college merged with the International Institute for Psychical Research, becoming the Institute for Experimental Metaphysics. It closed in 1947 and all its library and records were destroyed during World War II.

McKenzie paved the way for future study of psychic phenomena but there were allegations of mismanagement, fraud and hoaxing. He claimed that Houdini had genuine psychic powers. Houdini responded, "I do claim to free myself from the restraint of fetters and confinement, but positively state that I accomplish my purpose purely by physical, not psychical means."

McKenzie authored several pamphlets, and a book, *Spirit Intercourse: Its theory and Practice* in 1916. He said, "this book is written by a business man for business men and women on a subject which they have left too long in the hands of their religious teachers."

Chapter 6 is entitled First Steps to Spirit Intercourse. He gives advice to beginners that is still prudent today. He says," There is no one too simple, too young, or too ignorant, but may learn in a few days how he or she may consciously open up communication with the Spirit World."

He said that even though book learning can benefit the practice, they are not necessary to learn communication. Religious belief or affiliation does not matter. One can be Christian, Jewish, Buddhist or agnostic. He insists that one doesn't even have to have faith in the process to begin. It is a waste of time to delve into idle discussion about the process. Investigation and learning takes work and practice. "The proof of the pudding is in the eating."

Some may worry that it is dangerous to contact the Spirit World. McKenzie states that, "The earnest investigator is well protected by spirits of an intelligent order who stand vigilantly behind the veil." He does warn that the psychic science must be pursued with moderation, for any excess is always injurious.

He said that one must not confuse messages. Some may come telepathically from those still alive. A medium's own thoughts may mix with those of the spirit. Several spirits may attempt to communicate at the same time. He also warned that spirits often forget details of their earthly existence.

McKenzie reminds the reader that communication with the Spirit World is governed by natural laws. We may not understand those laws completely, but we can work with them. This is a science "not to be lightly entered into."

Additional Reading:

Boddington, Harry (1947, 1985) *The University of Spiritualism* London: Psychic Press.

https://www.scribd.com/document/82168750/Spirit-Intercourse-j-Hewat-Mckenzie

Vice-Admiral W. Usborne Moore: Unbeliever Turned Believer.

W. Usborne Moore spent 35 years in the British navy and commanded six surveying vessels before he retired. At that time, he was an agnostic and unfamiliar with beliefs outside the traditional churches. Looking for the truth, he began investigating mediumship in the early 1900s. He observed dozens of mediums in both Great Britain and the United States and reported his findings in two books: *"Glimpses of the Next State" and "The Voices."*

Moore said that his study of spiritualism was not the result of the search for a loved one who had passed. He simply wanted to get at the truth. He felt that as a surveyor, interested in detail, he was as qualified to investigate the subject matter. He explored both physical and mental mediumship.

Moore's first trip to America lasted one month. What he witnessed convinced him that those whom he had thought of as dead were very much alive. Medium Joseph B. Jonson of Toledo, Ohio, initially materialized his father and mother. "In these there was no possibility of error," Moore wrote. On February 1, 1909, Jonson manifested 10 spirits for Moore, including Moore's father, mother, and Lola, a deceased relative who appeared to him many times. Etta Wriedt of Detroit was so impressive, that Moore's book, *The Voices*, published in 1913 dealt solely with her mediumship

When Moore returned to England he wanted to persuade others that Spiritualism was not a delusion and could not be disregarded. What he discovered was that many others could not see or hear what he did. Their minds were unprepared. "They were both hostile to the subject, and their eyes and ears were open only to what their minds expected – which was nothing – or fraud," he said.

Moore did admit there was a great deal of fraud in the practice of mediumship. He said, "The temptations of these psychics are great; whatever powers they possess are sporadic and cannot be summoned at will; they find this out early in their development, and, in order to maintain regular séances, they learn the art of jugglery to 'help out' their particular gift at times when they feel they have not got their usual power."

Moore returned to America in December 1908. He spent two and a half months traveling to the cities of Rochester, Toledo, Detroit, and Chicago. He experienced automatic mirror-writing, materialization, direct writings, pictures precipitated by invisible intelligences, and direct voice. The evidence he obtained in these séances convinced him that he had directly communicated with Lola and with many relatives and friends.

Moore said that communication with the Spirit World is a complex process. Spirits may answer questions in a contradictory and misleading manner. He attributed this to the struggle in translating from one world to the next. "The difficulty of our spirit visitors in communicating at all must be enormous," he said. "We ply them with questions, the majority of which they are not able to answer because they have not yet reached the higher spheres; they make the attempt by stating what they have heard from others, and are, doubtless, often incorrect..."

The spiritualist Arthur Conan Doyle described Moore as "among the greatest of psychic researchers." Moore died March 15, 1918.

Additional Reading:

http://thegroundoffaith.net/issues/2009-06/AdmiralMoore.pdf

Moore, William Usborne (1913) *The Voices*. Reprinted 2011 White Crow Books

Eusapia Palladino: Physical Medium or Trickster?

Eusapia Palladino was born near Bari, Italy, in 1854. Her young life was filled with tragedy. Her mother died in childbirth and her father was assassinated by brigands 12 years later. As an orphan, she was hired by an upper bourgeoisie family in Naples as a nursemaid.

Her abilities became apparent when as a small girl she heard raps on furniture and saw eyes glaring at her from the darkness. While working as a nursemaid in 1872, she came to the attention of Signor Damiani, a noted Italian psychic investigator. Under his guidance, Eusapia's abilities progressed rapidly, first producing physical phenomena, then spectral appearances, including phantom limbs issuing from her body.

Her spirit guide, John King, communicated through raps and in trance spoke in Italian. She would also produce raps with upward movements of her head and her hand would cause the table to lift in the air.

One witness wrote in 1888, "Either bound to a seat, or firmly held by the hands of the curious, she attracts to her the articles of furniture which surround her, lifts them up, holds them suspended in the air like Mahomet's coffin, and makes them come down again with undulatory movements, as if they were obeying her will."

Senior Lombroso and Professor Tamburini examined her abilities to determine if she was a fraud. The professor held her hands and feet to prevent trickery. Lombroso wrote, "A handbell placed on a small table more than a yard distant from Eusapia sounded in the air above the heads of the sitters and then descended on the table, thence going two yards to a bed. While the bell was ringing we struck a match and saw the bell up in the air."

Over the years, Eusapia was tested many times in many countries. Some skeptics believed she was a trickster. One said he caught her in the garden gathering flowers to be used as "apports." Stanley LeFevre Krebs wrote a book exposing her tricks entitled *Trick Methods of Eusapia Paladino*. Magicians Harry Houdini and Joseph Rinn claimed all her feats were conjuring tricks. It is said that Eusapia even admitted to using trickery sometimes.

Others believed her abilities remained unexplained. In England, Madame and Pierre Curie treated séances as "scientific experiments" and took detailed notes. In 1905, Pierre reported on the testing done at the Society for Psychical Research, "It was very interesting, and really the phenomena that we saw appeared inexplicable as trickery—tables raised from all four legs, movement of objects from a distance, hands that pinch or caress you, luminous apparitions. All in a [setting] prepared by us with a small number of spectators all known to us and without a possible accomplice. The only trick possible is that which could result from an extraordinary facility of the medium as a magician. But how do you explain the phenomena when one is holding her hands and feet and when the light is sufficient so that one can see everything that happens?"

When Eusapia died in 1918, she left many followers and skeptics behind. We may never know the true extent of her abilities.

Additional Reading:

http://www.prairieghosts.com/palladino.html

McHargue, Georgess (1972). Facts, Frauds, and Phantasms: A Survey of the Spiritualist Movement. Doubleday.

Natale, Simone (2016). Supernatural Entertainments: Victorian Spiritualism and the Rise of Modern Media Culture. University Park, PA: Pennsylvania State University Press.

Coral Polge: Psychic Artist

Coral Polge was born in London in 1924. At the time of her birth, the midwife exclaimed, "This child has been here before." Maybe that is why she became a renowned psychic artist.

Most mediums and clairvoyants communicate with the Spirit World through thought messages, auditory, visual or even olfactory. Coral took that communication one step further by translating the images she saw onto paper. A trained commercial artist, she combined her artistic talent and psychic gift into a technique that enhanced the experience of reaching the Spirit World.

Unlike many mediums, Coral was not psychic as a child, though she did have a few out-of-body experiences. She also used to walk with her favorite uncle through the graveyard where she admired the stones and drew sketches of them. It was that same uncle who first sent her a message from the other side when she joined a spiritualist church at the age of 23.

Coral began her journey as a psychic artist by drawing medium guides. It wasn't until after she met Frank Leah that she realized she should be drawing pictures of loved ones who had passed. The perfect likeness of a loved one would convince a skeptic that life goes on, and that death is a new beginning. As she produced more evidential portraits of friends and relatives, she began to verify her work with photographs.

"Seek the truth," Coral's spiritual guides told her in her early days. She was always open to improving her technique.

Maurice Barbanell, editor of Psychic News, helped her by advising she demand a higher percentage of relatives come forward. She had never thought about demanding from the spirit people, but it worked. Artist, Samuel Martin, offered her advice to improve her artistry. He even returned after his passing to give her words of wisdom.

"I never had any doubts, once I start on the spiritual path, as to where I was going," she said. "I have never become disenchanted with my beliefs, only occasionally with the people involved. More than anything, spiritualism has given me a complete inner peace, to know a purpose manifests in everything."

In her book, Living Images, Coral relates the stories of some of the drawings that she created over the years. One is about the grandmother of Wendy Hart. While drawing the picture of a Victorian woman with hair pulled back from her face, Coral kept getting the word, sunshine. When Mrs. Hart found a photograph of her grandmother to compare to the drawing, she found that written on the back were the words "From your Sunshine."

Coral said that many of her communicators didn't explain the messages she was passing on. "We are purely telephone lines, nothing more," she said. "As long as there is somebody's picture waiting to be drawn, I will continue to be used as a channel for such communication between this world and the next. This was the path mapped out for me. It is a path I tread with love, and a great sense of privilege that I was chosen to do so."

Coral received the Spiritualist of the Year award in 1978 and died in 2001.

Additional Reading:

Polge ,Coral and Kay Hunter (1991) *Living Images*. The Aquarian Press, Harper Collins London.

Morris Pratt: Institute Builder

Born in 1820 in New York, Morris Pratt moved to Milton, Wisconsin and built a successful farm. After visiting Lake Mills Spiritualist Center in 1851, he became interested in psychic phenomena and Spiritualism. During the 1850s, he witnessed séances, spirit knockings, and the work of mediums.

He was known to argue frequently with ministers who criticized Spiritualism. On numerous occasions he was evicted from churches. One time, he was even fined for his actions. These conflicts led him to the realization that there was a need for educated individuals to present the religion in an intellectual way.

He vowed that if he were ever wealthy he would give his fortune to support the "scientific teaching of spiritual truths."

About 1884, Pratt invested his savings with Mary Hayes Chynoweth, a well-known psychic healer. Her spirit guide had instructed her to purchase acreage in the northern Wisconsin forests. The land, it turned out, contained some of the richest iron ore deposits ever found. Pratt eventually sold his shares for more than $200,000.

Pratt did not hesitate to fulfill his promise. In 1888, he began construction on the most expensive home in Whitewater, Wisconsin. The building was assessed at $30,000 and contained two large auditorium halls, one which seated nearly 400 people. Pratt designed the building as a temple and a school for Spiritualism.

In 1901, he filed a petition for incorporation of the Morris Pratt Institute. The subjects taught would be Science, Mathematics, Language, Oratory, Voice and Physical Culture, English and

Rhetoric, Bible Exegetics, Higher Criticism, Logic and Parliamentary Law, Comparative Theology and Psychic Culture.

Unfortunately, Pratt passed on to the Spirit World on December 2, 1902 before his dream came to fruition. Moses Hull, a Seventh Day Adventist minister who had turned to Spiritualism, went forward with Pratt's plans and opened the school on September 29, 1903.

Additional Reading:

Morris Pratt Website: http://www.morrispratt.org/

Paschal Beverly Randolph: African American Trance Medium

Paschal Beverly Randolph was born in New York City in 1825. His father was said to have been a member of the "Randolphs of Virginia." His mother, Flora, claimed to be the granddaughter of a Queen of Madagascar. She died before he was ten years old. Paschal was raised by his half-sister, Harriet, for a time before being passed on to an unidentified actress. He received less than a year of formal education, but spent time educating himself. As a teen, he took off on his own and spent about five years at sea before apprenticing as a dyer. He also worked also as a barber.

After converting to Roman Catholicism, Randolph investigated Spiritualism and became a trance medium. By his mid-twenties he had established a public career as a lecturer and writer. Like many Spiritualists, he fought for of the abolition of slavery. He took a leading role in recruiting Black soldiers for the Union army and in educating *Freedmen* in Louisiana during the Civil War. Afterward, he taught literacy to freed slaves in New Orleans.

Randolph traveled to England in 1853 and 1857 where he addressed the audiences as Sir Humphrey Davy and other well-known men. On later travels to France, Egypt and the Turkish Empire, he collected information on occult practices such as the magic mirror, hashish use and sexual magic. His teachings influenced many American occultists, including Madame Blavatsky and the Theosophical Society.

In addition to his work as a medium, Randolph educated himself to be a medical doctor and wrote and published more than fifty books, both fictional and instructive. His writings spoke of spiritual beings from other planets, of elemental creatures, the mysteries of the human aura, and the existence of seven universes, each with seven sub-parts, making forty-nine in all.

In 1861, he visited Paris where he became acquainted with a few reputed Rosicrucians. He began using the pseudonym "The Rosicrucian" for his Spiritualist and occult writings. Eventually, he founded the *Fraternitas Rosae Crucis* in 1858, and their first lodge in San Francisco in 1861.

Randolph lived in many places, including Boston, New York state, New Orleans, San Francisco, and Toledo, OH. He married twice. His first wife was African-American, his second wife Irish-American. He died in Toledo, Ohio, at the age of 49, under mysterious circumstances. Authorities claimed his death was the result of a self-inflicted gunshot wound to the head. Later, R. Swinburne Clymer, who became Supreme Master of the *Fraternitas*, confessed on his death-bed to killing Randolph in a state of jealousy and temporary insanity. Lucas County Probate Court records list the death as accidental.

Additional Reading:

Deveney, J P (1996) Paschal Beverly Randolph: A Nineteenth-Century Back American Spiritualist, Rosicrucian and Sex Magician. SUNY Press.

Charles Richet: Ectoplasm

Charles Richet was a French physiologist who was known for his work in immunology. He became a professor at the College de France in 1887 and taught neurochemistry, thermoregulation and homeothermy in animals. He won a Nobel Prize in 1913 for his research on anaphylaxis, the body's allergic response.

Richet's interests extended beyond the subjects of medicine and physiology. He wrote books about various topics including history and philosophy as well as plays and poetry. He was also an aviation pioneer.

Hypnosis and extrasensory perception were among the various topics that Richet investigated. He met medium Eusapia Palladino in 1884. That led to the founding of the *Annales des sciences psychiques* in 1891. He became the president of the Society for Psychical Research in 1905 and president of the Institut Metapsychique International in Paris in 1930.

Richet didn't believe in the afterlife or spirits, but he coined the term "ectoplasm" in 1894. He believed the substance was a material projected from the body of a medium, not from an otherworldly source. He considered the existence of spirits unscientific and preferred to believe extrasensory phenomena were related to a sixth sense.

He admitted that, "...although in certain rare cases spiritism supplies an apparently simpler explanation, I cannot bring myself to accept it. When we have fathomed the history of these unknown vibrations emanating from reality – past reality, present reality, and even future reality – we shall doubtless have given them an unwonted degree of importance. The history of the

Hertzian waves shows us the ubiquity of these vibrations in the external world, imperceptible to our senses."

Richet investigated the claims of several mediums, including Eva Carriere, William Eglinton, Pascal Forthuny, Linda Gazzera, and Eusapia Palladino. He was sure there was a physical explanation for paranormal phenomena and published a book, Our Sixth Sense, about the subject in 1928.

Additional Reading:

https://psi-encyclopedia.spr.ac.uk/articles/charles-richet

Theodate Pope Riddle: Pioneer, Architect and Spiritualist

Theodate Pope was born as Effie Brooks Pope, an only child born to Alfred and Ada (Brooks) Pope in Salem, Ohio in 1867. Effie changed her name to Theodate in honor of her grandmother, Theodate Stackpole, when she was 19. At the time, the wealthy family lived on Euclid Avenue ("Millionaires' Row") in Cleveland. She later graduated from Miss Porter's school in Farmington, Connecticut, and the family hired faculty members to tutor her privately in architecture.

Like other prominent professional women at the time, Theodate was interested in spiritualism and psychic research. She donated large sums of money to psychical research, believing in the endurance of the human spirit, but still skeptical about the validity of mediums' claims. She was on her way to London to gain support for an American chapter of the London Psychical Research Society with fellow enthusiast, Edwin Friend, when they became part of a bigger story.

Forty-eight-year-old Theodate had booked passage on the Lusitania, which departed New York on May 1, 1915 with 1,960 passengers and crew, bound for Liverpool. After being hit by a German torpedo, the ship sank in 18 minutes. Twelve hundred people perished, including Edwin Friend. Theodate jumped from the ship wearing a life ring and ended up clinging to an oar. When she was found, she was so lifeless that she was thought to be dead and placed with the other bodies. Fortunately, she was revived and returned home to further her architectural career.

A day shy of the one-year anniversary of Lusitania's sinking, Theodate Pope married John Riddle, a diplomat who had served in Russia. Theodate was best known for her design of Avon Old Farms School in Avon, Connecticut. She also designed other innovative private schools and a number of private homes, including the Hill-Stead estate, the Pope home in Farmington. Among her best-known architectural commissions was the 1920 reconstruction of President Theodore Roosevelt's birthplace in New York City.

By the 1920s, Theodate had established herself in her profession. The American Institute of Architects, which once declined her application for membership on the basis of her gender, now elected her a fellow.

Theodate lived through two world wars, times when spiritualism blossomed, and the Lusitania sinking. She contributed to the field of psychical research; took bold actions in the Spiritualist movement, established a notable career in architecture and fought for woman's suffrage. She passed away on 30 August 1946. Hill-Stead, is now a museum that not only showcases her architecture, but also her collection of artwork.

Additional Reading:

Katz, S L (2003) Dearest of Geniuses: A Life of Theodate Pope Riddle, Tide-mark Press.

Mary S. Vanderbilt: Devoted Spiritualist

Mary Scannell was born in Massachusetts in 1867. Her mother died when she was only three years old and she was raised by an aunt. It was 12 years after her mother's death that Mary had her first spirit vision. That was followed by a séance during which a Native American girl named Bright Eyes spoke through Mary. Bright Eyes requested that Mary remain in the house and train as a medium for three months.

Mary was reluctant to train as a medium, declaring that she and her aunt should move from their home, but she eventually gave in to the spirit's demand. Bright Eyes would speak through Mary for the next 34 years.

Mary spent her first six years holding private séances and tests as a medium. While married to her first husband, George Pepper, she worked with Abram H. Dailey to improve her grammar while under the spirit's influence. After that time, she conducted public demonstrations in New England, New York, Philadelphia, Washington and at conventions of the National Spiritualists' Association. She traveled extensively, including trips to Europe and Russia where she conducted "envelope readings."

After divorcing George Pepper, Mary married Edward Ward Vanderbilt in 1907, despite the objections of his family who insisted Mary as an unscrupulous fraud. Edward apparently adored her and encouraged her to work as a medium.

Mary was president of Lake Pleasant Camp in Massachusetts for five years. A 1916 Banner of Life publication stated that people came "in carts, in wagons, in anything, the Lord only knows how they all get there" to listen to Mary. It was common to have over

5000 people attend her demonstrations at Camp Etna, a Spiritualists' camp west of Bangor, Maine.

Mary continued to demonstrate her skills as a medium for seventeen years at Camp Etna and acted as its president the last 10 years of her life. After the 1918 summer season, Mary returned home and became ill. During her last address at the 71st anniversary of Modern Spiritualism in Berkeley Hall, she declared her devotion to Spiritualism, urging all to be true to the cause. Her last words in public were, "I have found Spiritualism a good thing to live by, and I have come pretty close to finding it a good thing to die by."

Her final illness passed quickly, and she died April 27, 1919 in Boston. In accordance with her request, her ashes were interred at Camp Etna.

Additional Reading:

Cadwallader, M E (1921) Mary. S. Vanderbilt: A Twentieth Century Seer. Reprinted by Digital Text Publishing Co. in 2011

Etta Wriedt: Spirit Voice Medium

Trance, Clairvoyance, Clairaudience, and automatic writing are all techniques used by Spiritualists to communicate with the Spirit World. A number of physical mediums were able to produce the phenomena called Direct Voice at the turn of the 20th century. The list includes Mrs. Everitt, Mr. Cecil Husk, Mr. CE Williams and George Spriggs, but one that stands out is Mrs. Etta Wriedt.

Etta was born in Detroit in 1859. She was a professional medium who only charged one dollar for a séance. She didn't sit in a cabinet, and never went into trance. Etta had two spirit guides. One guide was named Dr. John Sharp. He said he'd been born in Glasgow in the 18th century but moved to the US where he became an apothecary farmer in Evansville, Indiana. The other contacted Etta during her five trips to Great Britain. He was called John King or "Sir Henry Morgan" and he had lived in Britain 250 years before.

During Etta's visits, John King produced many physical effects. Flowers were taken from vases and handed to sitters, invisible fingers touched the sitters, luminous discs as bright as the moon moved around the inside of the circle. Sitters were also sprinkled with drops of water and wafted with cool air. Heavy objects moved around them. Etta clairvoyantly read names that were shown to her. When she called out the name, if it was recognized by one of the sitters, the name would be called through a trumpet.

Etta never went into a trance, so she talked naturally during all of her séances. She would give names and described spirit visitors and indicate for whom they had come to communicate with. Sometimes she would be interrupted by a spirit voice, and the two would talk simultaneously. Voices were heard in full-light as well as in darkness. Two, sometimes three, and rarely four voices were heard speaking at the same time about matters unknown to the medium. On one occasion one voice was singing while the other spoke. Etta only spoke English, but the voices spoke other languages such as Dutch, French, Spanish, Norwegian and Arabic.

Sir William Barrett said of her mediumship, "I went to Mrs. Wriedt's séances in a somewhat skeptical spirit, but I came to the conclusion that she was a genuine and remarkable medium, and has given abundant proof to others, beside myself, that the voices and the contents of the messages given are wholly beyond the range of trickery or collusion."

Admiral Usborne Moore made detailed records about the extraordinary mediumship of Etta Wriedt. "This American woman has a mysterious gift which enables those who sit in the same room with her to learn of the continued existence of those whose physical bodies have perished. The possession of this strange power is acquired by no virtue of her own; she was born with it," he said.

Additional Reading:

http://whitecrowbooks.com/michaeltymn/entry/was_etta_wriedt_the_best_medium_ever

Stemman, Roy (1972) *One Hundred Years of Spiritualism*. Spiritualist Association of Great Britain.

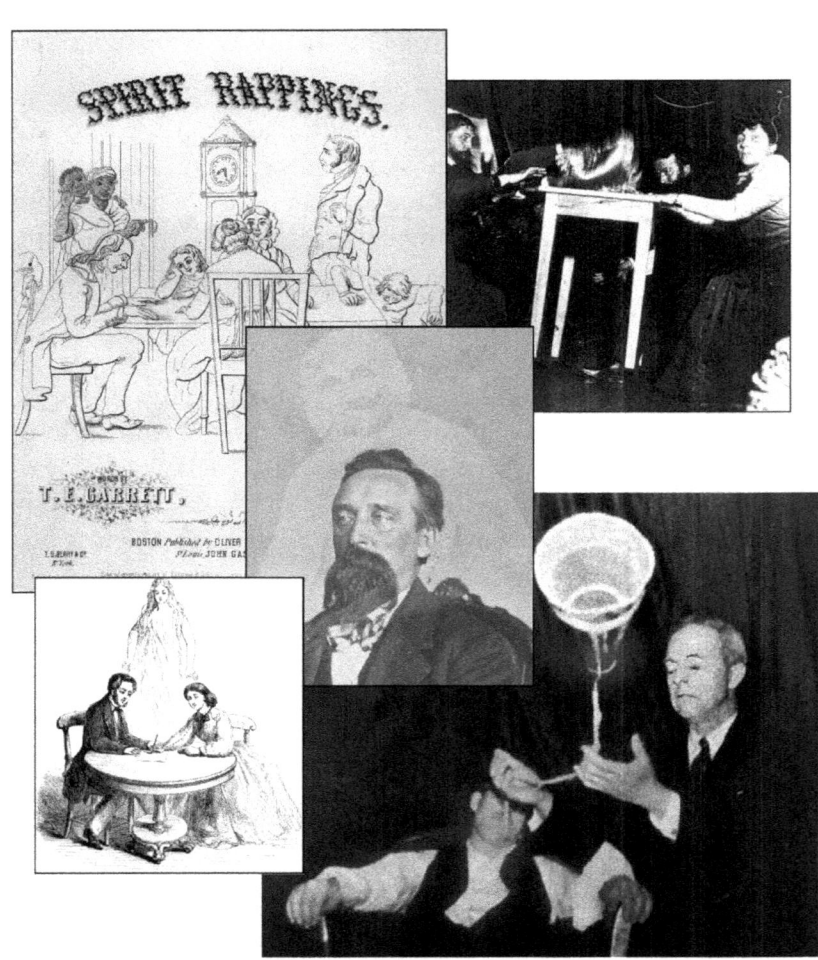

Section IV:

THE PRACTICE OF SPIRITUALISM

Finding your Silence

We all get caught up in the day to day activities of our lives. The house and car and clothes and phones and cable TV we thought we needed require more of our income than we had planned. Kids and pets and family members are always competing for our attention. The internet follows us during our waking hours, and we fall into bed exhausted each day. And don't even mention politics.

There's a saying; "The one who dies with the most toys wins." Is this all there is to life? An unending struggle for stuff? Rushing from one thing to the next? Being bombarded by news and advertisements and people wanting our attention? Is there no place to stop and examine life? Is there no sanctuary?

Spiritualism calls on its followers to find silence.

Silence is a sanctuary, a place to communicate with not only departed ones but with yourself. It might be found in a small room in a cabin on a mountain lake, a bedroom in a high-rise apartment, or a flower garden in the backyard. But it can also be found while sitting on a seat in a crowded bus, driving home on the highway, or while walking through the grocery store. Your sanctuary is internal and with you always.

H. Gordon Burroughs said, "We enter the sacred sanctuary to communicate with the inner self, the exhaustless, Everlasting Eternal part of ourselves. The I AM. This real person has always been and has passed through cycles upon cycles of manifestation, making a record of all experiences and manifesting now in this Objective form."

Spiritualism teaches that while we live in our physical body and create things in this world, we also create a temple in the invisible realm. No matter what we believe or what religion we embrace, this inner sanctuary is being created by our inner thoughts and actions, not by our outward manifestations. What type of temple are you building? Is it one with solid walls, a beautiful garden, and welcoming entrance. Or is it abandoned, desolate and rundown?

It is when we enter the silence that we take stock of ourselves and reach beyond our physical world. We achieve a high state of awareness in which we are open to true illumination. We discover how beautiful this sanctuary can become. Our consciousness becomes attuned to the real self. Infinite love understands the need of the individual. We find that we can build a temple of joy, hope, and tolerance. We realize that our purpose in being here is to learn, to accomplish, and to experience. We see the divine spark in every human being.

When you enter the silence, relax, listen, love, and receive. The troubles of the day will disappear, and your problems will dissolve. You will find that you are cared for, guided, and directed, and that you are living both now and for eternity.

Additional Reading:

Burroughs, H. Gordon (1962) *Becoming a Spiritualist*, Port City Press, Baltimore, Maryland

Forget Yourself and Grow

According to spiritualist H. Gordon Burroughs, "Every day is a new time; we have all eternity in which to grow, to become, to arrive in fulness and completeness."

It makes no difference how we arrived into this world, rich or poor, healthy or ill, wanted or unwanted, it is our choice to either hang on to the past and wallow in our condition, or to move ahead with what we've been given. Spiritualism teaches that no matter how long we have in this life or how we feel at this moment, we can leave all our mistakes in the past and begin anew.

Dwelling upon our past and present physical conditions often prevents us from doing worthwhile things and creating a better future. When we seek to use higher forces, we can put aside the lower or physical side of our life. According to Burroughs, "Spiritualism says to the so-called practical ones of earth, forget yourselves; lay aside that part of yourselves to which you have listened so long, that part which says, I cannot; I fear."

When seeking our spiritual self, our minds awaken to right and constructive thinking. We become receptive to the promptings of the "real" self. By leaving our ego behind, we can reach higher and perform greater achievements. With training, we can achieve power which removes all obstacles on our path of life. We find that our physical body is in harmony with the world. Ill health, unhappiness, and failure are cast aside. The spirit self knows no defeat and is a part of the All.

Pain and pleasure are part of human existence. Pain is the result of working against nature; pleasure is working in harmony with nature. We can endure pleasure longer then pain because it is harmonious, but both too much pain and pleasure can destroy our ultimate spiritual goal. Spiritualism teaches that we should enjoy everything in moderation. It is that moderation that allows for a happy existence on the earth plane and in Spirit World as well.

To be successful we should consider perseverance an ideal goal. Burroughs said Spiritualism teaches that "the secret of success lies in seeking high and right ends, and in embracing every opportunity of attaining them, never forgetful of the golden rule in whatever station in life it may please infinite intelligence to place us." Find what you do well, and do it unselfishly, without thought of reward or fame. Get rid of the ego. Selfish effort in time usually brings only failure.

Spiritualism also says to love and to be loved and respected during our short lives here. The goal is not to attain the most popularity or possessions. When we depart to the Spirit World, we should leave behind a well-rounded, useful life. The spark of Divinity that dwells within each of us should give us poise, receptivity, and sympathy. Love and kindness should be part of our daily life. This leads to true success.

Additional Reading:

Burroughs, H. Gordon (1962) *Becoming a Spiritualist*, Port City Press, Baltimore, Maryland

Angels in Our Lives

When I first became a medium, I focused on speaking with spirits. I believed there were angels but didn't consider communicating with them to be part of my work. I never encountered them until I began to familiarize myself with angels by studying and meditating about their existence. My study of angels opened my mind to them. One evening while I was sitting at home one came to me, not as a symbolic image in my mind, nor as an apparition, but as a scent. The entire room filled with lavender.

As I was thinking about my blog for this week, the topic of angels kept coming to mind. I had just received a book entitled *Angels in Action: What Swedenborg Saw and Heard* by Robert H. Kirven. He relates his connection to angels at different times in his life and discusses Emanuel Swedenborg who studied both the sciences and philosophy in the 1700s. Swedenborg's visions of the spirit world give us some understanding about angels and their purpose in the life after.

Swedenborg said that angels weren't supernatural beings. They are spirits of people who had lived on the earthly plane. "I have seen faces of angels of the third heaven so beautiful that no painters, with all their skill, could render a fraction of their light with their pigments or rival a thousandth part of the light and life that show in their faces," he said. According to him, angels have no halos or wings, but are clad in garments representing their stage of being, shinning with knowledge and wisdom. Swedenborg also said that angels have numerous tasks, each suited for their own special interests and abilities.

In his book, Kirven said that angels come to us to serve and assist us with our lives. They hear our appeals and will help lead us along our true path in life. Angels come to us from deep within our subconscious mind. Their help may come to us as a renewed sense of strength or a glow of affirmation. They could also come to us in dreams or meditative states. Sometimes they may appear when we are fully consciousness. They may even be heard as a voice.

Not everyone is going to experience a lavender scent filled room when an angel is near. Most encounters will be much subtler. Kirven said, "There's no easy way to distinguish with certainty between an emotion that is felt deeply, and a feeling induced by angelic influence." We must always be alert for the touch of an angel in our lives. They come to guide us and help us make our way through life. If we pay close attention, we will know.

Additional Reading:

Kirven, Robert H (1994) Angels in Action: What Swedenborg Saw and Heard, Chrysalis Books, UK

It's Supposed to be the Most Wonderful Time of the Year

As I was decorating the church the other day, Andy William's Christmas classic, *It's the Most Wonderful Time of the Year*, echoed through the sanctuary. Andy sang of good cheer, holiday greetings and gay happy meetings. But I knew that the season wouldn't be happy for everyone.

It's supposed to be a time when family and friends come to call, but how many people will be alone for the holiday? Maybe their job has taken them far from home. Maybe they are elderly, and their family and friends have all passed on. Maybe their expectations or family conflicts have isolated them from others. For these people, there will be no parties for hosting, no marshmallows for toasting, nor caroling in the snow.

It is during happy times when we are often so caught up in our own merriment that we overlook those who need us most. We forget the real reason for the season, to share with others, to give of ourselves. It's important to remember that not everyone is surrounded by large wonderful families. Some have problems during the holidays, and some are overcome with great sadness when they remember loved ones who are not with them. Many people have no one to spend these times with and are besieged by loneliness.

We all need caring thoughts and loving prayers. Those who have family problems, health struggles, job issues, or worries of any kind just need to know that someone cares. No one should be alone this time of year. The greatest gift you can give is your love and compassion.

When I opened the Spiritual Path Church, one of the first programs I started was a candlelight Christmas Eve service. I wanted people to feel welcome and at home. I wanted to offer them a loving haven where they would not be isolated on Christmas Eve. I invited everyone to come sit in the power of the angels. As a Spiritualist, I wanted them to understand that we are never alone, that there are always loved ones and angels watching over us.

It is my wish that the when anyone sits in this little Spiritualist church, they are surrounded by the glorious and magnificent feelings of love and endearment that come from their love ones and the angels. I know when I sit here on Christmas Eve, memories come back from days gone by. I am fortunate I have my congregation and family to share these wonderful feelings with.

I see a lot of lonely and distressed people this time of year for a variety of reasons. It is my obligation, no, my pleasure, to assure people that their love ones are still around in a spiritual form, and to help them with issues of closure. We must all be the light that helps others see. We must extend a warm and helping hand of compassion to a lost soul to bring their spirits back. By doing so, you will also create a gift of healing for yourself as well.

By giving love and compassion to others, you will make this the most wonderful time of the year.

Visiting a Medium: What to Expect

It's the medium's job to connect the earthly plane to the spiritual one. She is working for the Spirit World and not her own physical, egocentric, or financial goals. She is there to relay messages from the spirits of loved ones and those who have passed, and she can only communicate the information that is given to her. With this basic understanding, there are ways to improve the quality of a reading by taking several steps.

One: Keep an Open Mind. Your attitude toward a medium's reading can affect it as much as the medium's ability. It is important to have enough skepticism not to be taken in by frauds, but if your mind is closed, it will make communication for the medium more difficult.

Two: Calm your Fears and Anxiety. Obtaining a reading, especially for the first time, can be an anxious time. Some people fear what they will be told. Others fear that "evil" spirits will possess them or that contacting the Spirit World is a sin. You must put all these fears aside and clear your mind to be attentive and hear the messages that are coming to you.

Three: Establish Balanced Communication. When messages come from the spirt world, you must do your part. The medium cannot work in a vacuum and needs feedback to know if the communication is working. A response of, "Yes, that is correct," or "No, that is not right," or "Maybe, I don't know," will let the medium know if she has established the correct connection. This sort of feedback will improve the medium's interaction with the spirit and more information will come through. Even though it is good to respond, do not give the medium additional details. A simple yes and no are enough. The medium should be giving you a message, not the other way around.

Four: Have Realistic Expectations. Remember, a medium is working for the Spirit World. They are not a cell phone that you can use to call someone on the other side. The person you had planned on contacting might not be the one who contacts you. If that is the case, pay attention to the message you do receive. It is given to you for a purpose. The spirit may not want to discuss something of interest to you. Once a person crosses to the other side, their priorities change. What was important during their earthly life may not be important to them anymore. Again, listen to message.

Five: Take Notes. It is difficult to remember everything that is said during a reading. It is good to take a few notes, especially if it is a long session. Sometimes a message seems incorrect or out of place at the time. Information may need to be checked. Notes are helpful for future reference.

Six: The Right Medium. Mediums have their own distinctive styles and preferences. If you are uncomfortable with someone or feel they are not a good match for you, find someone else

Harry Edwards' Thoughts on Mediumship

As I was contemplating today's blog, I came across a book by Harry Edwards called *A Guide for the Development of Mediumship*. Edwards became a spiritual healer in 1936. His early attempts at spiritual healing were met with some success. Gradually, his fame spread. He moved to Surrey just after WWII and used the front room of his house as a healing sanctuary.

In his book, he wrote that it's not necessary for a person to have an extensive education or training, or to be versed in psychic science, to become a medium. There are many instances of simple folk becoming outstanding mediums and healers.

He does insist that mediumship be approached with the right goals in mind. Many people wish to become mediums to speak with the spirit people to obtain counsel, to heal the sick, to help the bereaved, or to give advice and assistance to those who are in need. Others wish to become mediums to satisfying their own egos, to be different from other people, or to command respect. Self-promotion and aggrandizement should be prevented at all costs. The medium is not there for their own goals, but to demonstrate the existence of the spiritual world.

Edwards reminds us that Spiritualism came into being to reveal to man that he is not just a physical being. Man is part spirit and life is an apprenticeship for a greater and fuller life that commences with physical death. It is by receiving spiritual knowledge that mankind will receive and adopt an enlightened code of values that will lead to the end of war, poverty and other troubling trends in our present world. The medium's true motive is a spiritual one. If this is not the case, then it is fruitless for spirits to use humans as instruments for the progression of souls.

Students of mediumship should possess an inner yearning to be used for the higher purpose, and to view mediumship as a means to help others. It should be a denial of selfishness and a giving of self to a spiritual purpose. A true medium becomes a participant in the divine plan for the furtherance of good. Mediumship needs a mind that is strong, purposeful and capable of self-discipline.

Mediumship was born as an exact Spirit Science, but it cannot be assessed by analysis or material values; it cannot be put under the microscope. Because of our inability to fully comprehend the science of mediumship, an air of mysticism has surrounded it, and this has at times given rise to questionable practices and opinions. It has been attacked, ridiculed and opposed, but still survives. As understanding of the process evolves, it becomes more respectable and acknowledged by scientists, religious leaders, and the press.

Today, there are a great number of classes being held in Spiritualist churches and in-home circles. The mediums who conduct these are sincere, good people, but it is understandable that all sorts of practices have arisen. These practices have been handed down from medium to medium, and have become accepted as being true, when in fact they may not be. The overlap between mediumship and psychic readings has also increased, leading to a blurring of goals and expectations.

One must remember that a medium's true goal is spiritual, to be a conduit between the physical and spiritual worlds, to stand as an example to others and to be proof of man's spiritual nature. Without that goal, one is neither a Spiritualist nor medium."

Additional Reading:

Edwards, Harry (1998) A Guide for the Development of Mediumship, Spiritual Truth Press

https://www.bookdepository.com/publishers/Spiritual-Truth-Press

Beginning Mediumship

Although some people have more natural talent than others, all psychics and mediums need to develop their skills. This takes patience and practice. Patience cannot be stressed too strongly, especially today when we expect everything to be instantaneous.

There is no set of instructions that works for everyone. We are all individuals and need to approach mediumship in our own unique way. There are general principles that we can all follow.

Be serious: Training to become a medium is not a game or frivolous task. You need to approach the mission with an open mind and serenity.

Be patient: Those with a natural talent may see results in a short amount of time, but others may take weeks or months to develop their abilities. Be prepared to practice for as long as it takes.

Stay healthy: Mediumship does not require a special diet or physical training, but it's best to maintain your health to develop the energy required to connect with the Spirit World.

No sign is too small: Don't expect large physical manifestations, disembodied voices, or knocking sounds when you first begin. It takes time to develop a connection with the spirit world, and signs will start out small.

Keep regular hours: Chose a time of the day for your training. It doesn't have to be exact, but within a few minutes of the same time each day. Begin with a ten or fifteen-minute meditation session every other day to start. Gradually increase the time that you are sitting until it's about 30 minutes. Daily sessions are acceptable, but don't go beyond that as a beginner.

Set aside a training room: Select a room that is quiet and not too large. The light should be subdued. Red cloth can also be put over a lamp light to shade the harshness. Training can be done in the dark, but you will need to keep from falling asleep. Sit in a comfortable chair.

Practice *Expectancy*: Sit quietly and clear your thoughts of worldly concerns. Put yourself in a receptive mood. Be alert, but don't expect anything. Just wait.

Stay calm: Normal physical responses to sitting include points of light appearing because of eye strain in a dark room, creaking floor boards or furniture, and numbness in arms or legs because of stiffness. Don't over react to these and miss genuine light phenomena or raps that do occur.

Developing A Mediumship Circle: Part 1

Natural psychics are much more common than mediums. Many use their abilities without training, but even natural mediums can benefit by developing their innate gifts. Therefore, it's important to have disciplined mediumship circles available to help individuals achieve greater awareness and control over their abilities.

Three people may constitute a circle, but to train a medium seven is preferred. The Spiritualist's National Union suggests that training circles be composed of a Leader, Medium, Circle Recorder, Novice Medium and four Sitters. Each person has their own task to preform while the circle is in session.

Circles should not be held in rooms that are constantly used, because discordant vibrations could be present. Draperies and rugs should be avoided because they absorb power from the room. The ideal location should be empty except for a light wooden table and plain but comfortable chairs. The temperature should be moderate, so it does not distract. The air should be well ventilated to maintain an adequate oxygen supply.

The Leader makes absolute decisions about what happens in the circle. This person should have extensive training and knowledge and be able to observe and analyze what's happening during the session. Other members of the circle must follow the leader's instructions, unless of course, they are asked to go against their own principles or moral code. The Leader will be given instructions by the spirits through the Medium but evaluate all directives before proceeding.

The Medium will assist in maintaining communication and cooperation with spirt guides or operators. When a Novice

Medium is present, the Medium will advise the Leader about the psychic conditions and help the Novice by inducing mediumistic power. The medium should not be the Leader of the circle.

The Circle Recorder is appointed by the leader to sit outside the circle and take notes on all the proceedings. A tape or video recorder may be used instead if the spirits have no objections.

The Novice should show some indication that she is endowed with psychic ability and spiritual aptitude to begin mediumship circle training. The novice will learn under controlled circle conditions to "tune in" to the spirit frequency level. As she learns to respond to the psychic forces of a controlling spirit, she will develop a relationship with the spirt, who will become one of her guides.

The Sitters provide power for the circle. For novice development, four Sitters are preferred. They should be harmonious and healthy, but it is not a requirement that they have special psychic abilities. They must agree to participate for the sole purpose of providing energy to the Medium and Novice. They must refrain from pursuing their own development at that time.

Additional Reading:

Awrty, Marilyn. *Sunflower Series,* Booklets 1-4, Shen-men Publishing

Developing a Mediumship Circle: Part II

In Part 1, I discussed how to use a Mediumship Circle to train a novice medium. Other types of less formal Mediumship Circles can also be used to communicate with the spiritual world. These include open and closed, and Church and Home Circles.

Closed Church Circles give church members an avenue in which to practice elevating their vibrational connection to the Spirit World. The same individuals attend the circle at regular intervals, probably weekly. It's important to have a circle Leader who handles the administrative details. Circles should have a qualified Medium, and sitters should enter the circle with a positive frame of mind.

Open Church Circles encourage people to experience Spiritualism outside of a formal church service. Since these circles are open to anyone, the church must have a qualified and capable leader to run the group. The leader should introduce the circle with a few words about the philosophy of Spiritualism. Because there may be individuals who are unfamiliar with the process, the leader should explain the purpose and expectations of the circle to them.

It is the responsibility of the leader to ensure that messages are delivered as briefly as possible so that all may have a turn. Healing should not be offered without permission. Demonstrators should not work in trance conditions so that newcomers aren't confused. The leader makes sure that no one oversteps their bounds and that the circle is held in a respectful manner.

Home Circles date back to the origin of Spiritualism, when friends gathered in homes to communicate with the spiritual world. Today's home circles work in much the same way. A group of acquaintances gather at regular intervals to contact the Spirit World. These circles can be closed or open.

The Closed Home Circle is composed of the same individuals. They meet with the purpose of expanding their consciousness and improving their ability to connect with the spiritual world. Mediums will be able to improve their ability to unfold latent mental and physical abilities under these conditions.

Physical Mediumship: A new resurgence?

Physical mediumship was fairly common in the early half of the 20th century but waned over the last 80 years. Recently, it appears to be making a comeback. Mediums are advertising their abilities to communicate with the Spirit World and produce physical manifestations during demonstrations.

Physical Mediums provide an interface of communication between our world and the Spirit World. They can manifest energies and energy systems created by spirits. The processes result in physical displays, such as loud raps and noises, materialized objects or apports, materialized spirit bodies, or body parts such as hands, legs and feet. Other physical phenomena that can be produced are physical smells, hot or cold drafts, levitation, transfiguration, spirit lights, and direct voice communication.

True physical mediumship is believed to be very rare because of the bodily toll it takes while allowing spirits to materialize. Substances are taken from the medium's body to form what is called ectoplasm and photoplasm. Because the process can be draining, or even physically painful, physical manifestations were usually created under the direction of groups or circles of people, rather than a single medium.

Another reason for the rarity of physical mediumship is the fact that the development of the process can be a lengthy and tedious, with no materializations happening in a circle for months or years. It requires an extended commitment on everyone's part and may focus around one or two people providing the necessary energies or vibrations, while others contribute to the energies.

Because physical mediumship is rare and the potential for fraud is high, Arthur Findlay College has high standards and recommends eight points for evaluating mediums and conducting sessions where physical manifestations are expected. They are summarized here:

1. No séances or circles should be held in total darkness. Subdued colored lights or natural lighting is preferred. The use of infra-red cameras is suggested.
2. Mediums are required to be tested by the college before claiming to be a physical medium
3. Rooms used should be prepared and cleaned to remove ectoplasm, clutter and metal.
4. It is important for sitters to vocally respond to the medium.
5. No sitters should be allowed to bring electronic devises into the room.
6. Entrances to the room should be monitored at all times.
7. Physical mediumship is not entertainment and should be respected as a means of connecting with the Spirit World.
8. The medium should inform the sitters what to expect before the session.

Physical Mediumship can be an important tool to demonstrating the existence of the Spirit World but can be misused as a means of entertainment and financial gain. Silver Birch, spirit guide to Maurice Barbanell, explained it this way:

"Whether manifestation of the spirit is seen or heard does not matter very much. What is more important is the unfolding of your souls' power, for, as you sit here week after week, so you are attuning yourselves to higher vibrations and becoming more accessible to the wisdom of your ages, which is always waiting to pour itself down into your world of matter, to obey the law of service. But it must find instruments attuned to its vibrations.

And, as your souls unfold and you rise higher and higher in the scale of vibrations, so you come into closer touch with higher and greater spiritual forces, that are not seen or heard but which belong to the eternal realities of the spirit. That is the reality of your lives. So much of your time is spent in chasing the shadows, in trying to capture the illusion, in trying to secure the ephemeral. In silence, in harmony and in love, your souls unfold all the time. Though it may be slow, it is sure and certain.

Additional Reading:

Austin, A.W. (1998) *Teachings of Silver Birch*, Spiritual Truth Press, UK

Reading Auras

Charles Leadbeater, a member of the Theosophical Society, was the first person to popularize the concept of auras. In his book, *Man Visible and Invisible*, published in 1903, he illustrated the human aura at various stages of spiritual evolution. In 1910, he incorporated chakras into his book, *The Inner Life,* by combining old teachings with his own ideas. Leadbeater's concepts were later adopted by others such as Rudolf Steiner and Edgar Cayce.

Spiritualists define the aura as a type of electromagnetic energy that radiates from all physical objects. Living beings manifest a personal energy field that reflects their own unique spiritual vibration. As a physical body and spirit change, so does the aura. Some people are born with the ability to see or sense auras without training. Others may learn to develop the ability. It is through clairvoyance that a medium attunes to the spiritual vibrations of others.

Clairsentience can be used to sense a person's aura either in the physical plane or Spirit World. It may be on an emotional level, where one is determining their state of feeling. Are they happy or sad, or sensitive or aloof? Their mental energy can also be determined. This is the way their physical mind works. Are they intelligent or easily confused, or paranoid or trusting? The condition of the physical body can be determined as well. A healthy body will radiate a completely different energy than it does when it is sick. A well-trained medium will be able to detect subtle changes in the physical body that are not typically noticeable.

Since the aura is a type of energy, specific vibrations are sensed as colors by the human mind. One does not have to see the color, or even have working vision, to perceive the vibrations of the aura. Different colors may have different meanings, but there are basic guidelines one can follow:

RED: Passion or anger, energy and self-confidence, materialism.

ORANGE: Pride, the need for excitement, personal power and control.

YELLOW: Bright and cheery, intellectual and creative, sense of humor.

GREEN: Competitive and individualistic, processes ideas and information quickly, natural healers.

BLUE: Loving and nurturing, balanced, inspirational, noble, intuitive.

PURPLE: Wise, self-mastery, highly evolved and intuitive.

Other colors include pink (loving and gentle), white (pure and spiritual), and gray (dark thoughts).

There are many exercises you can try to develop your ability to sense auras. I'll describe one you can do at home. Position yourself a few feet away from something that is dark in color, like a curtain or piece of furniture. Hold your hands up, palms facing you, fingers slightly apart. Stare at your hands, letting your eyes go unfocused. After a while, you'll see a subtle glow around your hands. Once you see that, keep working. You will next see energy radiating from the fingertips. It will flow like wisps of smoke connecting the fingers of one hand to the fingers of the other. That is your aura.

Once you identify your own aura, you can try your ability on others, with their permission of course. It will take time and patience to develop your skills. Keep in mind the colors listed above while practicing. Once a person is adept at sensing the auras of physical persons, the same technique can be used to identify spirit auras. Colors will enable you to describe the spirit in more detail when conducting readings for a client.

Additional Reading:

Leadbeater, Charles (1903) *Man Visible and Invisible*, Reprinted by Createspace 2008.

Trance Mediumship

Trance mediumship is a method used to allow a spirit to interconnect directly through a person's physical body. The medium needs intense focus to induce the trance state. It is important to put the ego aside for the communication to be delivered because the medium may influence the message with his or her own bias. The spirit or spirits using the medium's mind must be free to influence the thoughts being conveyed. Because the medium may not recall of all the messages given while in the deep trance state, an assistant is usually employed to record the session.

In the 1860s and 1870s, trance mediums were common in the Spiritualist community. Since it was a time of changing social standards, mediums delivered passionate speeches on women's suffrage, temperance and abolitionism.

Leonora Simonds Piper, born in Nashua, New Hampshire in 1859, was a popular trance medium. Her first psychic experience occurred when she was eight years-old while playing in the garden. She felt a sharp pain in her right ear and a voice whispered, "Aunt Sara, not dead, but with you still." She ran into the house and told her mother. Later, they discovered Aunt Sara had died the same day.

Piper's mediumship began in 1884 after her father-in-law took her for a medical consultation with J.R. Cook, a blind clairvoyant known for his psychic cures. Piper lost consciousness at Cook's touch and entered a trance of her own. From that time on, she dedicated her life in the service of Spiritualism, doing trance reading in both the United States and England.

Piper's talent was so notable that she traveled to England to be tested by the premiere psychical researchers of the day. Piper did extremely well and was accepted as genuine. Despite that, claims of fraud followed her when she arrived back in the United States. She traveled to England again in 1906 and took part in the complex network of medium communications known as cross correspondences which were successful. That did not stop the accusations of fraud. When she died, her abilities were still doubted by many.

Today, scientific testing is being more controlled and measured. In 2012, preliminary research by Julio Peres and his research team was conducted on trance mediums to examine changes in brain function with emission computed tomography. Their study investigated psychography, where a spirit writes through the medium's hand. They tested ten subjects, five less expert mediums and five with substantial experience, in both dissociative trance and non-trance states. They found lower activity in several areas of the brain in experienced mediums while in trance.

"This first-ever neuroscientific evaluation of mediumistic trance states reveals some exciting data to improve our understanding of the mind and its relationship with the brain," Andrew Newberg said. "These findings deserve further investigation."

Additional Reading:

http://journals.plos.org/plosone/article?id=10.1371/journal.pone.0049360

Apports and Asports

The psychic or spiritualist term, apport, is derived from the French word, *apport*, meaning the "action of bringing" or a "thing brought." An apport is an object that has been transferred from an outside place into a séance circle or room and is associated with poltergeist activity or séances. An asport is just the opposite. In this case, the object vanishes and is found elsewhere. Objects can range from inanimate things such as jewelry or coins, to living organisms like flowers or live animals.

The first recorded observation of an apport appeared in the *Researches psychologique ou correspondencesur le magnetisme vital entre un Solitaire et M. Deleuze,* published in 1839. Dr. G. P. Billot witnessed a dove flying around the room during a séance. It dropped a packet on the table. Inside, Billot found three pieces of paper with a small bone glued to each. Beneath was written, "St. Maxime, St. Sabine and Many Martyrs."

Marchioness Centurione Scotto, member of an old Genoa family, held séances in Millesimo Castle. At one séance a pair of earrings transported into the room following the appearance of a trumpet with a phosphorus band. The trumpet turned its large end up to fit against the ceiling. The earrings dropped into the instrument with a thumping sound.

Reverend C.L. Tweedale was a clergyman and author of an important psychic work, *Man's Survival After Death*, published in 1921. He reported numerous cases of objects appearing out of thin air. He described an incident which involved his mother, wife and himself. His wife had just parted his mother's hair to examine a wound. In the opposite corner of the room a jar of ointment which had been locked away in a chest in another room appeared. Apparently, it was to be used as a treatment.

More recently documented apport experiences were reported during the Scole Experiments which took place in the 1990s in England. For the objects to appear in their closed cellar testing room, they would have to pass through the walls, and maybe even through time. The Scole Group reported that "the arrival of an apport was announced by the sound of a loud thud, either on the floor or on the table."

The first apport was a coin, a Churchill Crown, which appeared in October 1993. During the next month, a silver thimble, two small silver lockets, a silver chain bracelet, and a St. Christopher medallion were among some of the apports that appeared. More than 70 apports in all were received during the Scole Experimental sessions.

One apport which created a great deal of discussion among the researchers was what appeared to be a new looking copy of the *Daily Express* newspaper, dated Monday 28th May 1945. It was printed on the type of paper used in the early- and mid-1940s with ink used at the time, but there was no sign of the usual yellowing which would have occurred if it was original. Interestingly, just a few weeks after the paper appeared, although carefully stored away from light and air, it turned yellow.

Additional Reading:

Solomon, Grant (2006) The Scole Experiment: Evidence for Life After Death, Campion Books

Traveling Clairvoyance

Clairvoyance is the ability to obtain information about an object, person or location through extrasensory perception. One form of clairvoyance is remote viewing or traveling clairvoyance. This is the ability to view locations from a distance. Psychics use remote viewing to gain information about places. Mediums are led by spirits to view distant locations as a means of confirming information for their clients.

Clairvoyance was reportedly used by primitive shamans and medicine men. A case of spontaneous traveling clairvoyance happened to Apollonius of Tyana, a Greek philosopher who died in 100 AD. While lecturing in Ephesus, Turkey, he suddenly stopped and informed the class that the tyrant Domitian had been killed in Rome. In 1756, Emanuel Swedenborg, who resided in Gothenburg, Sweden, had a vision of a fire devastating Stockholm. The Great Stockholm Fire occurred in 1759, reducing about 20 blocks containing 300 houses to ash, and rendered about 2000 persons homeless.

The Didier Brothers, Alexis & Adolph, French clairvoyants who practiced in the mid-1800s, read closed books, recover lost objects, and practiced traveling clairvoyance. President Pierre Seguier of France experienced their abilities. Alexis described Seguier's room and mentioned that there was a bell on the table. The President was unsure about the bell, but when he arrived home, found it had been placed on the table while he was away. In 1847, at the request of Marquise de Mirville, magician Jean Eugene Robert-Houdin, paid two visits to the Didier brothers. He tested them and confirmed their abilities.

Both Andrew Jackson Davis, 19th Century Spiritualist, and Edgar Cayce, 20th Century Clairvoyant, used traveling clairvoyance to diagnose their clients' health. Jackson said he was guided by the ancient Greek physician, Galen. Considered by some to be the father of modern holistic medicine, Edgar Cayce's readings created a detailed set of spiritual principles, healthful tonics, beneficial oils, and rejuvenating remedies.

During the 1970s, the U.S. government funded a project at Stanford Research Institute, to study remote viewing. Harold Puthoff and Russell Targ conducted a series of studies to determine whether participants could identify and describe the features of remote locations. Their first publication in Nature, March 1974 reported some degree of remote viewing success. David Marks and Richard Kammann were unable to duplicate their results and believed Puthoff and Targ may have inadvertently given clues to their subjects. The government study was cancelled in the 1990s.

As a technique used by mediums, traveling clairvoyance is a more advanced technique than reading spirit messages. It must be perfected with diligence and practice. Some people may be more naturally gifted at the practice than others, but it is possible for most to learn.

Additional Reading:

Davis, Andrew Jackson (1847), *The Magic Staff,* Essex: SNU Publication (Facsimile 1996)

Davis, Andrew Jackson (1847), *The Harmonial Philosophy,* London: William Rider and Son Ltd.

Edgar Cayce Website: https://www.edgarcayce.org/

Arriving in the Spirit World

English Spiritualist Medium, Ivy Northage, was known for her teaching abilities at the Ivy Northage School for Mediums. She took a no-nonsense approach to training, and many of her students became highly successful mediums. Ivy demonstrated clairvoyance and transfiguration early in her career. For well over forty years, she served churches, and taught at the SAGB (Spiritualist Association of Great Britain), and the College of Psychic Studies.

Ivy's spirit guide, Chan, gave hundreds of inspirational trance lectures. He used a practical and comprehensive approach to spiritual development. Many of his teachings were recorded and his teachings remain relevant today.

Chan had much to say about the transition from the physical world to the spiritual plane. He first explained that the ease of transitions depends upon the manner of death. For the person who is elderly or who has been sickly for an extended period, the passage is expected. During times of sleep or unconsciousness, the spirit leaves the body "while the silver cord which links the spirit body to the physical gradually becomes thinner and thinner." A slow and gradual transition can take place.

Those experiencing a sudden death may not be aware that they are dead for some time. If the person is in an accident, he might think he has miraculously escaped. He will tell the spirits greeting him that he is feeling fine. Because of the shock, he imagines surroundings that look identical to those on Earth. He sees himself still dressed in the clothes he was wearing. When spirit guides help him, he may believe he is being taken to a hospital. It isn't until the deceased notices that things are not quite normal, that the illusion begins to dissolve.

Chan refers to the astral belt of communication as a condition of higher vibration, not an actual physical location. Because a spirit can create the illusion of still being on the physical plane, he might not want to accept that he has passed. The spirit receives "spiritual first-aid" at this time and is gradually weaned away from his emotional attachment to his earthly existence.

Some spirits may choose to stay in familiar surroundings, creating houses and surroundings that they are comfortable with. This depends upon how attached they were to their physical life. The length of time that it takes a spirit to move beyond this stage is highly dependent upon the individual. At some point, the spirit will quicken its vibration and move beyond the emotional astral vibration that is closest to the Earth.

Additonal Reading:

Northage, Ivy (1993) Journey Beyond: Trance Talks by Chan, Spirit Guide of Ivy Northage. Light Publishing, UK

Connecting from the Spirit World

Most often, we focus on methods and techniques to connect our Earthly plane to the Spirit World. We don't realize that the spirits must work to connect from their side as well.

In the book, *The Blue Island*, William T. Stead describes his process of reaching Earth from the spirt world. He first brings up the issue of time. On earth we are acutely conscious of the passage of time. The Earth's orbit around the sun creates years. Its rotation divides those years into days and nights. People have subsequently divided days into hours, minutes and seconds.

He informs the reader that the Spirit World has no such passage of time. "We have no dark sky," he said. "only a light one, and we have, for the sake of the present illustration, an unlimited supply of energy. We do break up our time, but it is not your breaking, therefore we can seldom be accurate in telling when a thing did, or when a thing will, happen."

William Stead wrote of many buildings being present in the part of the Spirit World in which he resided. One of those buildings was used to establish communications with the Earth. He said that it was a well-organized, very business-like place. There were hundreds of people there trying to get messages back home to loved ones. He referred to the messages as "heart calls."

William said he expected the building to be equipped with different instruments to aid their communications but found none. "It was only the human element," he wrote. Connection was achieved by thought.

On his first visit to the building, he had a long conversation with a mundane looking man. He was told that they had a system of travelers who worked very closely with the Earth. "They had the power of sensing people who could and would be used for this work at the other end."

William visited the building frequently, trying to get messages home by more than one means. Sometimes he succeeded; sometimes he did not. "The spirit has much to do himself with the success or failure attained; a great deal depends upon him. Every time I succeeded I helped another." When he did fail, he was given unlimited help by those working there.

His first successful communication was with a group of people holding a séance. "I had to visualize myself among these people in the flesh. Imagine I was standing there in the flesh, in the center of them, and then imagine myself still there with a strong light thrown upon me....Create a picture."

The first time, none of his family were present and he made only his face visible to them. Later on, William Stead became adept at communication, and through spirit writing, gave us the information contained in the book, The Blue Island.

Additional Reading:

Woodman, Pardoe and Estelle Stead (1922) The Blue Island: experiences of a new arrival beyond the veil. Hutchinson & Co., London.

Available at: https://archive.org/details/blueislandexperioostea

What is Spiritual Healing?

First and foremost, Spiritual Healing is used to compliment traditional medicine. It is not considered an alternative. If a person has medical issues and is under a treatment regimen, they should continue seeing their physician. Spiritual Healing will work in concert with general medical practices.

Spiritual healing is more comprehensive than medical treatment. While traditional medicine works only on the physical body, Spiritual Healing is more Holistic. It can work on all levels of the self, thus treating the entire person.

An individual receiving Spiritual Healing doesn't need to have faith in the healing process. It can work on individuals that don't understand faith, like babies, young children and even animals. The more open and accepting the patient is to the process, the more successful the healing will be. Like with traditional medicine, the patients attitude can also affect the outcome. The more positive a person is, the better the chance of recovery.

There are three types of Spiritual Healing. The first is Contact Healing. Contact Healing involves the Medium Healer placing their hands directly on the patient's body. This is always with permission and may involve just a light touch on the shoulders. Each Medium Healer has their own way of working. A trained Medium will be aware of where they may and may not place their hands, respecting sensitive area. The Medium Healer will work under a Code of Conduct issued by their organization to which they must adhere.

The second and third healing types occur without touch. In Distant Healing, the healer and patient may be in the same room. Healing is sent by the power of thought. In Absent Healing, the patient is not physically present. Healing thoughts are sent to them.

The duration of the healing session varies depending upon the Medium Healer and the patient. It usually lasts between ten and twenty minutes. During the session, the patient is asked to relax and quiet their mind and may close their eyes to assist the process. As healing proceeds, the person may feel a little warmer or cooler, or there may be no change at all. Despite the initial response to the healing process, it may take time and several sessions for the healing effects to be noticeable.

Additional Reading:

Taylor, E. *A Psychology of Spiritual Healing* available at https://swedenborg.com/product/a-psychology-of-spiritual-healing/#full

Recommended Reading

Austin, C., D. Hopkins & B. Oates (2013), *The Philosophy of Spiritualism*, The Spiritualists' National Union iBooks.

Awtry, Marilyn J. (2011), *Spiritualism on the Move*, Shen-men Publishing

Awtry, Marilyn J. (2012), *Living in the Light*, Shen-men Publishing

Barbanell, M. (1936), *They Shall Be Comforted*. Psychic Press, Ltd.

Barrow, L. (1986), Independent Spirits Spiritualism and the English Plebeians 1850 - 1910. London: Routledge

Bassett, J. (1990), 100 Years of National Spiritualism. London: HCP

Bassett, J. (1992), *On the Side of Angels* Essex SNUP

Boddington, H. (1947, 1985), *The University of Spiritualism* London: Psychic Press

Braude, Ann (2001) Radical Spirits: Spiritualism and Women's Rights in Nineteenth Century America. Indiana University Press, Bloomington, IN

Burns, J. (editor) (8th March 1889), *The Medium and Daybreak*.

Burroughs, H. G. (1962), *Becoming A Spiritualist*. Port City Press

Cadwallader, M.E. (1922), *Hydesville in History*. Chicago: Progressive Thinker.

Cardace G. (1989), Willing Suspension of Disbelief Victorian Reaction to Spiritlist Phenomena in www.loyno.edu.iThistory/journal/1989-0/gregory.html

Carrington, H. (1930), *The Story of Psychic Science* London: Rider

Carroll, B. E. (1997), *Spiritualism in Antebellum America*. Indiana: Indiana University Press

Chryssides, G. (1999), *Exploring New Religions* London: Cassell

Davis, A. J. (1847), *The Magic Staff,* Essex: SNU Publication (Facsimile 1996)

Davis, A. J. (1847), *The Harmonial Philosophy,* London: William Rider and Son Ltd.

Doyle, A. C. (1926), *The History of Spiritualism* USA NY: George H Doran Company

Evans, W. H. (1917), *Constructive Spiritualism*. Two Worlds Publishing Co. Manchester, England

Findlay, J. A. (1951) *Where Two Worlds Meet*. Spiritualist National Union.

Findlay, J. A. (2010) *On the Edge of the Etheric: Survival After Death Scientifically*. Book Tree

Frank, A. R. (1853), "The Spirits come to Town, " *Chambers's Edinburgh Journal* (21 May 1853) 321-4

Guillory, M. S. (2016), Conscious Concealment: The Repression and Expression of African American Spiritualism. In *Histories of a Hidden God: Concealment and revelation in Western Gnostic, Escoteric and Mystical Traditions*. Ed. April D. DeConick & Grant Adamson. Routledge, London.

Heagerty, N. R. (2016), Portraits from Beyond: The Mediumship of the Bangs Sisters. White Crow Productions, Ltd.

Higginson, G. (1993), On the Side of Angels: Authorized Life Story. Tudor Press.

Jacobs, C. F., and A. F. Kaslow (1991). The Spiritual Churches of New Orleans: Origins, Beliefs, and Rituals of an African-American Religion. Knoxville: University of Tennessee Press

Lewis, E. E. (1848) A Report of the Mysterious Noises Heard in the House of Mr. John D. Fox in Hydesville, Arcadia, Wayne County. Authenticated by the Certificates and Confirmed by Statements of the Citizens of That Place and Vicinity. Power Press of Shepard and Reed, Rochester, NY

Maudsley, H. (1879), *The Pathology of the Mind* London: Macmillan & Co 2nd ed., 1868 McKenzie B in *Psychic News,* 10 August 1940 London: Psychic Press

McKenzie, J. H. (1917) *Spirit Intercourse: Its Theory and Practice* at: https://www.scribd.com/document/82168750/Spirit-Intercourse-j-Hewat-Mckenzie

Nelson, G. K. (1969), *Spiritualism and Society* London: Routledge & Kegan Paul

Oppenenhemi, J. (1985), The Other World Spiritualism and Psychical Research in England 1850-1914 London: Cambridge University Press

Owen, A. (1990), The Darkened Room Women Power and Spiritualism in Late Victorian England USA Philadelphia: University of Pennsylvania Press.

Ozten, T. (Editor) in Psychic News, Issue no 3706 July 12 2003.

Podmore, F. (1902), *Modern Spiritualism: A History and a Criticism, 2 Vols.* 1:112 , 123-4, 141 -153. London: Methuen

Polge, C. and K. Hunter (1997), *Living Images: The Story of a Psychic Artist.* Spiritualist Association of Great Britain.

Price, H. (1945), *Poltergeist Tales of the Supernatural* pp. 81-109 London: The Guernsey Press Co Ltd

Roach, P. (2004), *Wandering Between Two Worlds: Victorian England's Search for Meaning* http://www.gober.net/victorian/reports/mesmersm.html (Accessed 29 01 2004)

Russel, M. and C. R. Goldfarb (1978), *Spiritualism and Nineteenth-Century* London RMT

Solomon, G. (2006) The Scole Experiment: Evidence for Life After Death, Campion Books

Stainton, M. (1883) *Spirit Teaching* London SPR

Swedenborg, E. (2000), *Heaven and Hell: New Century Edition.* Translated by George F. Dole. Swedenborg Foundation.

Swedenborg, E. (2010), *Secrets of Heaven, Volume 1 & Volume 2, New Century Edition.* Translated by Lisa Hyatt Cooper. Swedenborg Foundation.

Underwood, P. (1986), *Queen Victoria's other World.* London: Harrop LTD

Wallis, E. W. and M. H. Wallis (1903), *A Guide to Mediumship and Physical Unfoldment.* Chicago, IL. at http://spiritwritings.com

Washington, P. (1993), Madame Blavatsky's Baboon: Theosophy and the Emergence of The Western Guru London: Seeker and Warburg

Woodman, P. and E. Stead (1922), *The Blue Island: experiences of a new arrival beyond the veil.* Hutchinson & Co., London at: https://archive.org/details/blueislandexper

www.ingramcontent.com/pod-product-compliance
Lightning Source LLC
Chambersburg PA
CBHW071312110426
42743CB00042B/1329